Matthew Lopez

THE INHERITANCE

Matthew Lopez is the author of *The Whipping Man* (Luna Stage Company, Manhattan Theatre Club), *The Legend of Georgia McBride* (Denver Center for the Performing Arts, Manhattan Class Company, Geffen Playhouse), *Somewhere* (The Old Globe, Hartford Stage Company), *Reverberation* (Hartford Stage Company) and *Zoey's Perfect Wedding* (Denver Center for the Performing Arts). In London, he was represented in Headlong Theatre's 9/11 Decade anthology with his play *The Sentinels*.

MATTHEW LOPEZ

The Inheritance

inspired by the novel Howards End by
E.M. FORSTER

FABER & FABER

First published in 2018
by Faber and Faber Ltd. 74–77 Great Russell Street
London WC1B 3DA

This edition with revised text, 2018

Typeset by Country Setting, Kingsdown, Kent CT14 8ES
Printed in England by CPI Group (UK) Ltd, Croydon CR0 4YY

A CIP record for this book is available from the British Library

978-0-571-35236-4

For Brandon

The Inheritance was originally commissioned by Hartford Stage (Darko Tresnjak, Artistic Director; Michael Stotts, Managing Director). The world premiere was performed in London at the Young Vic, Part One on 2 March 2018, and Part Two on 9 March 2018. The cast, in alphabetical order, was as follows:

Young Man 7 / Jasper Hugo Bolton
Young Man 5 / Charles / Peter / Agent Robert Boulter
Young Man 10 / Toby Darling Andrew Burnap
Young Man 3 / Young Henry / Tucker Hubert Burton
Henry Wilcox John Benjamin Hickey
Morgan / Walter Paul Hilton
Young Man 1 / Adam / Leo Samuel H. Levine
Boy Sam Lockhart, Joshua De La Warr
Young Man 6 / Tristan Syrus Lowe
Young Man 2 / Jason 1 / Paul / Doorman Michael Marcus
Margaret Vanessa Redgrave
Young Man 9 / Eric Glass Kyle Soller
Young Man 4 / Young Walter / Clinic Worker Luke Thallon
Young Man 8 / Jason 2 / Other Agent Michael Walters

Direction Stephen Daldry
Design Bob Crowley
Light Jon Clark
Sound Paul Arditti and Christopher Reid
Music Paul Englishby
UK Casting Julia Horan CDG
US Casting Jordan Thaler CSA and Heidi Griffiths CSA
Associate Director Justin Martin
Dramaturg Elizabeth Williamson
Dialect William Conacher
Fights Terry King
Assistant Director Sadie Spencer

Executive Producer David Lan

This production was supported by Nattering Way LLC
and Sonia Friedman Productions.

Andrew Burnap, John Benjamin Hickey and Samuel
H. Levine appeared with the permission of UK Equity,
incorporating the Variety Artistes' Federation, pursuant
to an exchange programme between American Equity
and UK Equity.

Sadie Spencer was supported by the Jerwood Assistant
Directors Programme at the Young Vic.

The Inheritance transferred to the Noël Coward Theatre in the West End of London, with a first performance of Part One on 21 September 2018 and of Part Two on 28 September 2018. The cast, in alphabetical order, was as follows:

Young Man 7 / Jasper Hugo Bolton
Young Man 5 / Charles / Peter / Agent Robert Boulter
Young Man 10 / Toby Darling Andrew Burnap
Young Man 3 / Young Henry / Tucker Hubert Burton
Henry Wilcox John Benjamin Hickey
Morgan / Walter Paul Hilton
Young Man 1 / Adam / Leo Samuel H. Levine
Young Man 6 / Tristan Syrus Lowe
Boy Harrison March-Ward, Anthony Zac Moran, Joshua De La Warr
Young Man 2 / Jason 1 / Paul / Doorman Michael Marcus
Margaret Vanessa Redgrave
Young Man 4 / Young Walter / Clinic Worker Jack Riddiford
Young Man 9 / Eric Glass Kyle Soller
Young Man 8 / Jason 2 / Other Agent Michael Walters

Direction Stephen Daldry
Design Bob Crowley
Light Jon Clark
Sound Paul Arditti and Christopher Reid
Music Paul Englishby
UK Casting Julia Horan CDG
US Casting Jordan Thaler CSA and Heidi Griffiths CSA
Executive Producer David Lan
Associate Director Justin Martin
Dramaturg Elizabeth Williamson
Dialect William Conacher
Fights Terry King
Resident Director Jane Moriarty

The Young Vic production was presented in the West
End by Tom Kirdahy, Sonia Friedman Productions and
Hunter Arnold with Elizabeth Dewberry & Ali Ahmet
Kocabiyik, 1001 Nights Productions, Greg Berlanti,
Brad Blume, Shane Ewen, Rupert Gavin, Robert Greenblatt,
Marguerite Hoffman, Mark Lee, Peter May, Arnon
Milchan, Oliver Roth, Scott Rudin, Tulchin/Bartner
Productions, Bruno Wang, Richard Winkler, Bruce
Cohen/Scott M. Delman.

Characters

E. M. Forster ('Morgan')
Eric Glass
Toby Darling
Walter Poole
Adam McDowell
Henry Wilcox
Leo
Margaret

Young Man 1
Young Man 2
Young Man 3
Young Man 4
Young Man 5
Young Man 6
Young Man 7
Young Man 8
Young Man 9
Young Man 10
Tristan
Jasper
Jason 1
Jason 2
Charles Wilcox
Paul Wilcox
Tucker
Toby's Agent
Clinic Worker
Doorman
Toby's Other Agent

THE INHERITANCE

Hidden

From all I did and from all I said
they shouldn't try to find out who I was.
An obstacle was there and it distorted
my actions and the way I lived my life.
An obstacle was there and it stopped me
on many occasions when I was going to speak.
The most unnoticed of my actions
and the most covert of all my writings:
from these alone will they come to know me.
But perhaps it's not worth squandering
so much care and trouble on puzzling me out.
Afterwards – in some more perfect society –
someone else who's fashioned like me
will surely appear and be free to do as he pleases.

Constantine Cavafy (1908)
translated by Daniel Mendelsohn

Part One

Prologue

A handful of Young Men sitting around writing.
Some with pencils on paper, some on laptops, a few on
typewriters. Off to the side, apart from the group, one
lone young man sits. We shall call him Young Man 1.

Young Man 1 He has a story to tell – it is banging
around inside him, aching to come out. But how does
he begin? He opens his favorite novel, hoping to find
inspiration in its first familiar sentence. And in reading
those words, he finds himself once again in the gentle,
reassuring presence of their author.

An older man enters. He is E. M. Forster. We, like all
his intimates, shall call him Morgan.

Morgan I hope I'm not disturbing you.

Young Man 2 ⎞ No, please!

Young Man 6 ⎟ Join us!

Young Man 5 ⎬ You're not disturbing us at all.

Young Man 7 ⎠ We could use the distraction.

Morgan How's the work coming?

They groan in frustration.

Young Man 2 ⎞ It's going terribly.

Young Man 3 ⎟ I hate everything I've written today.

Young Man 4 ⎬ I'm a total fraud.

Young Man 5 ⎠ Others have said this better than I ever
will.

Young Man 6 } I have nothing original to say.

Young Man 7 } All my work is derivative.

Young Man 8 } My characters won't do what I want them to.

Young Man 9 } I've been writing this same sentence for seven hours.

Young Man 10 I think I'm a fucking genius.

Morgan (*to Young Man 1*) Why aren't you writing?

Young Man 1 I don't know how to start. I thought that maybe I'd read a little and see how others begin their stories.

Morgan You have stumbled across the writer's most valuable tool: procrastination.
  What is your story about?

Young Man 1 Me. My friends. The men I've loved. And those I've lost.

Morgan Goodness me. Friendship, love, loss. Sounds like you're off to a very good start.

Young Man 1 But the thing is I'm not! My ideas refuse to become words.

Morgan Yes, I understand. All your ideas are at the starting post, ready to run. And yet they all must pass through a key-hole in order to begin the race.

Young Man 1 I picked up one of your books –

Morgan Which one?

Young Man 1 hands the book to Morgan.

Young Man 1 *Howards End.* 'One may as well begin with Helen's letters to her sister.' God, what a great first

8

sentence! So dashed off, as if to suggest it doesn't really matter how you start.

Perhaps it doesn't.

Young Man 1 I keep returning to this book again and again.

Morgan Tell me: what is it about the novel that speaks to you? What do you find in its pages?

Young Man 2 Guidance?

Young Man 8 Compassion.

Young Man 4 Wisdom.

Young Man 5 I love its humanity.

Young Man 7 Its honesty.

Young Man 1 It comforts me.

Young Man 10 Not me. I mean, it's a great book, don't get me wrong. And the movie's good. But, I mean, the world is so different now. I can't identify with it at all.

Young Man 9 It's been a hundred years.

Young Man 7 The world has changed so much.

Young Man 3 Our lives are nothing like the people in your book.

Morgan How can that be true? Hearts still love, don't they? And break. Hope, fear, jealousy, desire. Your lives may be different. But the feelings are the same. The difference is merely setting, context, costumes. But those are just details.

Young Man 1 All I have are details. What I don't have is a beginning.

Morgan Why do you need to tell your story?

9

Young Man 1 To understand it. To understand myself.

Morgan That's a story I'd like to hear.

Young Man 1 Will you help me tell my story? Our story?

Young Man 7 Who we are.

Young Man 6 How we got here.

Young Man 4 And what we mean to each other.

The Lads encourage him.

Morgan I would be delighted.
So, to begin: who does your story start with?

Young Man 1 Toby.

Morgan One may as well begin with Toby's . . . what?

Young Man 1 Voicemails.

Morgan One may as well begin with Toby's voicemails –

Young Man 1 – to his boyfriend.

Act One

Summer 2015–Summer 2016

SCENE ONE

1. A Party at the Hamptons

Young Man 10 becomes Toby Darling.

Young Man 1 *Beep!*

Toby You are going to *die* when I tell you what you're missing. Call me back.

Young Man 1 Toby's had a martini. *Beep!*

Toby Where are you? You can't be asleep already. You are missing the most *exquisite* party, holy shit! Call me when you get this. God, I love the Hamptons!

Young Man 1 Toby's had another martini. *Beep!*

Toby Okay. So. First of all this house is *gorgeous*. It's this sleek, modernist saltbox, all concrete and glass with a massive infinity pool that stretches out to the ocean. And all of it so tastefully decorated, you would *die*.

Young Man 1 And its owner, Henry Wilcox?

Toby Oh, Henry Wilcox! You were right: Henry Wilcox is really kinda dreamy. I want to be him when I grow up. He's wearing the most magnificent suit, which was made by this Savile Row-trained tailor on the Upper West Side. And when I asked him for the guy's information, Henry says:

Young Man 1 'Oh Toby, he's way out of your price range.'

Toby Which is such a dick thing to say and yet coming from the mouth of Henry Wilcox, I was simply *dazzled*.

Oh! And we played football today. Tackle, not touch. Can you imagine me playing football?

All the Lads No!

Toby Well, I didn't. But I could have if I wanted and that's the point.

Young Man 1 And Henry's partner: Walter Poole?

Toby Oh, Walter! How do I describe Walter?

The Lads help him out with suggestions.

Walter has this sort of, I don't know, this ghost-like spirit about him. Like a sheer curtain in front of an open window. He's like Valium. I love him.

Holy shit, Meryl Streep is here! Eric, this party is *ridiculous*. Call me back!

Young Man 1 Toby's had five martinis. *Beep!*

Toby Walter just said I could stay the whole weekend! Pack a bag, bring me some underwear, and get your ass on a train first thing tomorrow morning. You are going to love it here!

Young Man 1 New York City is a Darwinian experiment. Every summer, waves of college graduates wash up on its shores to begin the struggle toward success and achievement.

Young Man 5 They are young, ambitious, intelligent and driven –

Young Man 8 Also helps if they're attractive.

Young Man 6 – each convinced they have the talents and abilities not just to survive in the city –

Young Man 2 But also to thrive.

Young Man 1 Toby Darling and his boyfriend Eric Glass were two such strivers.

Morgan Let's have a look at them.
   Right. So . . . neither were all that young anymore –

Toby Hey!

Morgan – nor particularly brilliant –

Eric Wait a second.

Morgan – or successful –

Toby Oh come on!

Morgan And yet, through no enterprise of their own, they were the inhabitants of an enormous three-bedroom, two-bathroom apartment with a terrace that overlooked the park on the fifteenth floor of an elegant pre-war building on the Upper West Side of Manhattan.

   Young Man 9 becomes Eric Glass.

Morgan Eric Glass was packing a bag just as Toby walked into the apartment –

Young Man 1 Hungover and miserable.

2. *Eric and Toby's Apartment*

Toby Hey.

Eric Toby? I was just about to head to Penn Station.

Toby Didn't you get to my voicemail?

Eric You left two dozen.

Toby The one from early this morning.

Eric No, I guess I / didn't –

Young Man 1 *Beep!*

Young Man 2 Hey, it's me.

Young Man 3 It's early.

Young Man 4 Like, maybe six?

Young Man 5 Look, change of plans.

Young Man 6 I'm taking the first train back.

Young Man 7 And please delete all my messages from last night.

Young Man 8 I wish I'd never come.

Eric What happened?

Toby I am so humiliated. I can never show my face there again. I can never leave this *apartment* again.

Eric Just tell me, babe.

Toby I threw up.

Eric Oh. That's not so bad. On the train?

Toby At the party.

Eric Oh. Well . . . like . . . on the lawn / or –?

Toby On their sofa.

Eric Oh.

Toby And their dog.
      Which was sitting in Meryl Streep's lap.

   The Lads react.

I am beyond mortified. Alec Baldwin and Mariska Hargitay watched me *projectile vomit* over *the most transcendent and celebrated actors of all time!!*

Eric It's not like it was Glenda Jackson or anything.

Toby You've seen *Sophie's Choice*! I am so humiliated.

Eric Oh Toby. So what happened then?

Toby Everyone fled the room like I had *Ebola*. Meryl Streep just sat there, covered in vomit. The dog, it . . . Oh God, the dog started . . .

Eric Just tell me –

Toby It started licking it off her face.
   Are you laughing?

Eric Not *at* you.

Toby Thank *God* for Walter, who acted as if this sort of thing happens *all the time* in East Hampton. He helped the most nominated actor in Oscar history up and out of the room. Then he brought me a ginger ale and helped me up to my room. I woke up around five and Ubered over to the train station before the sun came up.

Eric You left without saying goodbye?

Toby Well, I wasn't going to stick around for breakfast!

Eric Oh Toby . . .

Toby What are you doing?

Eric I'm calling Walter.

Toby No, please!

Eric We can't just say nothing.

Toby Yes we can! I promise they'll forget all about us by next week.

Eric I don't want them to forget about us. I like Henry and Walter.

Toby Well I promise you they don't like us anymore. Just please let it be.

   Eric reluctantly puts his phone away.

God, I'm such a mess.

Eric You've puked all over this city and lived to show your face again.

Toby But never in the Hamptons. Everyone at that party was so cool and unaffected, like they belonged there.

Eric They *did* belong there. Maybe someday we'll belong there, too. Or maybe that's just not us and we'll belong somewhere else.

Toby But no it *has* to be us. You didn't see that house, Eric. (*Then, truly bummed.*) Aw. You didn't see that house. I'm sorry I ruined our beach vacation.

Eric It was a plan for all of a minute. I barely had time to cancel anything. In fact, I was planning to noodle around the Whitney today. Maybe go to Film Forum. You wanna come?

Toby I'm so hungover, babe. I just wanna fall asleep and wake up in my forties.

Eric Oh Toby.
   Go to sleep. I'll be home to make you dinner.

Toby Call me before you head to the movies. I might just rally.

Morgan What does Eric do now?

Young Man 1 I think he calls Walter anyway.

Morgan And who is Walter?

Young Man 1 You are.

   Morgan becomes Walter Poole.

Walter Hello?

Eric Hi, Walter? It's Eric Glass.

Walter Well hello, Eric Glass. I wondered if I might hear from you today.

Eric Yeah. So listen, about last night, Toby feels just awful.

16

Walter Judging from the number of martinis Toby had, I'm not surprised.

Eric Listen, are you sure there isn't something we can do? I can send a check / or maybe call a –

Walter What you can do is to put it out of your mind.

Eric Well . . . I'll try.

Walter Now if you'll excuse me, the steam cleaners have just arrived. Totally unrelated to the events of last night, I assure you. So nice to hear from you, Eric.

He hangs up, becomes Morgan again.

Morgan Eric Glass opened his home regularly to his friends.

Young Man 1 He cooked elaborate dinners for all the fascinating people he collected over the years, listening to their stories –

Morgan Rarely offering his own in return.

Young Man 1 And so it was, on Friday, October 9, 2015 that Eric Glass opened his home to his friends to celebrate his thirty-third birthday. He served dinner, poured wine, and played for them a piece of music that had recently captured his ear.

End of Scene One.

SCENE TWO

October 9, 2015. Eric's Thirty-Third Birthday

1. Eric and Toby's Apartment

Eric and Toby with a group of four other young men. Ravel's String Quartet in F Major plays.

Eric Toby and I heard a group from Juilliard playing this afternoon at the Strand.

Tristan Who's it by?

Eric Ravel.

Jason 2 I don't really know Ravel. What's he done?

Jason 1 What do you mean, 'done', babe?

Eric 'Bolero'.

Jason 2 Which one's that?

Eric has to start dah-dah-dahing 'Bolero'.

Oh right! Torvill and Dean. And he wrote this?

Eric Yes.

Tristan It's so captivating.

Eric Isn't it?

Jason 2 I think I once heard this in a movie.

Jasper Yeah, me too. *Atonement*, maybe?

Jason 2 Or *English Patient*? Something English.

Jason 1 Maybe *The Talented Mr Ripley*?

Jason 2 Oooh! We should totally watch that again.

Eric Here, let me skip to the second movement.

He skips ahead in the piece.

Isn't that nice? I love all that plucking.

Toby Eric's into hard-core plucking.

Tristan It sounds like the bubbles in a glass of champagne.

Eric Yeah, I hear that.

Jason 2 Or a bumblebee racing around a meadow.

Eric Yeah, I hear that too. All right, I'm gonna check on dinner.

Young Man 1 Excuse me.

Eric Hey, babe, can you open another bottle of wine?

Toby Absolutely.

Young Man 1 Um, excuse me?

Tristan What are you making? It smells so good.

Eric I got this enormous leg of lamb at Dickson's.

Young Man 1 enters, carrying a bag from the Strand.

Young Man 1 Excuse me. I'm so sorry to interrupt your party. Do you remember me?

Eric No.

Young Man 1 I was sitting next to you today at the Strand. Do you remember me?

Eric Sorry . . .

Young Man 1 When they were playing that music? Do you remember me?

Eric Umm . . .

Toby Oh yeah, the twink who asked us what piece they were playing.

Young Man 1 Yes.

Jason 2 It's Ravel.

Eric And now you're here.

Young Man 1 Yes.

Toby Why are you here?

Young Man 1 It's, um, my bag.

Toby The bag in your hands?

Young Man 1 No, that bag over there.

He points to another Strand bag on the floor.

I think you took my bag.

Toby What?

Young Man 1 Accidentally. We both had our bags on the floor and when you left, I think you may have grabbed mine. Accidentally.

Eric Oh my God, we are so sorry. Toby, you did again!

Jason 1 'Again'? You mean he's done this before?

Eric Constantly! He's always taking things that don't belong to him. Scarves, gloves, umbrellas.

Jasper Virginity.

Eric Seriously baby, you're becoming a real kleptomaniac.

Toby I didn't even notice.

Eric We are so sorry about that.

Young Man 1 You're Toby Darling, right? You wrote the book *Loved Boy*?

Jasper	Oh wow, that just happened.
Tristan	Toby, you just got recognized.
Jason 1	That's pretty cool.
Jason 2	You're famous!

Toby Is that how you recognized me? You read my book, it changed your life, you saw me in the bookstore and so you followed me home for an autograph, making up a story about switched bags?

Young Man 1 Actually, you left your wallet in the bag.

The Lads die laughing at this.

Also . . .

He removes five copies of the same book from the bag he brought in.

Jason 1 Is that your book, Toby?

Jasper You bought six copies of your own book?

Tristan Oh Toby, you crack me up.

Toby Yeah, laugh it up, guys. If you must know, I promised the ladies on the ninth floor that I would bring them each a signed copy for their book club.

Eric Have you read Toby's book?

Young Man 1 No, but I –

Jason 2 So what books did *you* get?

Jason 2 grabs Young Man 1's bag.

Young Man 1 Oh, I'm –

Jason 2 A Cavafy collection.

Eric Ooh, which translation?

Jason 2 Mendelsohn.

Eric The best.

Jason 1 ⎫ I've been meaning to get that. Let me see.

Jasper ⎭ What else has he got?

Jason 2 *Giovanni's Room. Call Me by Your Name. The Swimming-Pool Library.*

Jason 1 I'm sensing a theme here.

Toby You're buying all these queer books, why didn't you buy mine?

Tristan Because you'd already bought every copy in the store, Toby.

Jason 2 You should turn it into a movie, Toby.

Jason 1 Yes! It would make a great movie!

Toby Actually – (*To Eric.*) Should I tell them?

Eric It's your news, babe.

Toby Yeah, but nothing's official yet.

Jason 1 Oh wow, he *is* turning it into a movie!

Toby No, *but* – I have been commissioned to turn it into a play.

Silence. Then –

Jason 2 A musical?

Toby No, a straight play.

Eric (*off 'straight'*) Well . . .

Jason 2 Will there be any music in it?

Toby I don't know, I haven't written it yet.

Jason 1 I could totally see it as a play, Toby.

Toby Thank you.

Tristan Toby, that's amazing. / Congratulations.

Jasper Yeah Toby, good for you.

Toby Thank you. I'm really excited.

Eric ⎱ It's going to be an amazing play.
Jason 2 ⎰ Just be sure to put some music in it.

Toby (*to Young Man 1*) Do you want to take a copy?

Young Man 1 You don't have to / give me –

Toby Would you read it or would you just throw it on a shelf?

Young Man 1 No, I'd read it.

Toby Then it's your book.

Young Man 1 Thank you. I should let you get back to your / party.

Eric No, stay.

Jason 2 It's Eric's birthday!

Young Man 1 Happy birthday.

Eric Thank you. Are you hungry? I made tons of food.

Young Man 1 Oh, I couldn't –

Tristan Eric is an amazing cook.

Eric Or maybe a glass of wine? We were just listening to the piece they were playing at the Strand

Young Man 1 Oh God, I really loved that piece.

Eric Yeah, me too. It's beautiful, isn't it?

Young Man 1 Yeah. It . . . it yearns.

Eric Yes it does! That is the perfect word. I think it's about mourning.

Young Man 1 Oh interesting.

Eric You don't agree?

Young Man 1 I think . . . I think maybe it's about unrequited love.

Eric Really? How?

Young Man 1 It's romantic but in a way that feels unresolved.

Jason 2 Funny, I don't hear that at all.

Young Man 1 Maybe I'm wrong.

Toby Don't let them bully you.

Young Man 1 Okay. Well, in the first movement, the phrases are legato, rising and falling, like breath – no – like a sigh. I imagine someone looking at photos of someone they've loved for a long time. There's sadness in the music. Then the second movement starts with plucking instead of bowing. It's summery and fresh. It makes me think of a butterfly flitting through a meadow.

Jason 2 I said a bumblebee.

Young Man 1 But then halfway through the second movement, the sadness returns, as if our character suddenly sees the object of their desire in the flesh. That painful, yearning feeling that comes when you want someone so badly and you know you can never have them. Then the last movement is really agitated, like a raging fire that completely consumes the person. Burned alive by their own desire.

Silence, then:

Toby A raging fire? You got all that from listening to it once at a bookstore?

Young Man 1 That's just the way my brain works.

Eric You're not drinking your wine.

Young Man 1 Oh, I don't / really –

Eric Do you want something else?

Toby Maybe something stronger?

Young Man 1 Oh, no / I –

Eric I could make you a cocktail.

Toby Eric makes a mean Manhattan.

Jason 2 Ooh, I want a Manhattan!

Tristan Yeah, me too.

Toby Eric, you have been commissioned to make Manhattans.

Eric Yes! On it!

Tristan (*to Young Man 1*) You're gonna be crawling home, I promise.

Toby So what's your story, kid?

Jason 1 } Are you in school?

Jason 2 } How old are you?

Tristan } Where are you from?

Jasper } Do you have a boyfriend?

All eyes on Young Man 1.

Young Man 1 I should probably go.

A great protest from the Lads.

Eric Oh no, stay. Please.

Toby They're harmless, don't mind them.

Eric We've got tons of food, lots of good wine.

Young Man 1 No, I should go. Thank you, though.

Eric Will you come back, then? Now that you know where we live?

Young Man 1 Thank you. I . . . thanks.

Young Man 1 grabs his bag, exits. Eric looks at his guests.

Eric You are all just the worst.

Tristan Don't look at me.

Jasper We just asked him about himself.

Eric You couldn't have made him feel just a little more welcome? Did you hear how he talked about that piece of music? And we chased him away.

Toby So look him up on Facebook.

Eric Yes! Good idea, Toby. What was his name?

They all stare at each other blankly.

We didn't think to ask him his name.

Toby Who wants a Manhattan?

2. *Eric Interlude*

Morgan Eric Glass did not keep many secrets. But there was one truth he kept to himself, even from Toby.

Eric What truth is that?

Morgan Eric Glass did not believe he was special. He was not as brilliant or as accomplished as his friends. He thought of himself – in all things and in all ways – as painfully ordinary. What he did possess in place of these qualities was a profound vivacity, a continual and sincere response to all that he encountered in his path through life. Whilst admiring the fearlessness in others, he was, in his own life, cautious.

Eric Eric had taken the first job he was offered out of college, working for his friend Jasper, whose brilliance he glimpsed from their earliest days as classmates as Yale.

26

Jasper Jasper started his own company at the age of twenty-one, working as a social justice entrepreneur. Eric was his first employee.

Eric He met Tristan his first year after college. They went on three dates and decided –

Young Man 6 – they were each other's best friend. Tristan is a physician.

Eric He works in the emergency room at NYU Medical Center.
    Eric met Jason while working as volunteers on the Kerry campaign in 2004.

Young Man 8 We lost that election. But the friendship remains. Jason is a first grade teacher.

Young Man 2 Yes! And his boyfriend –

Young Man 8 No, his partner –

Young Man 2 His partner, whose name is / Stephen –

Young Man 8 – also named Jason –

Young Man 2 Right, his partner, also named Jason is a / human rights –

Young Man 8 – is a high school science teacher.

Young Man 2 Yes, okay fine. BUT – they're not just partners –

Young Man 2 pulls out two wedding bands from his pocket. Young Man 2 slips a ring onto Young Man 8's finger.

They're married.

Morgan To each other?

Young Man 2 Yes, of course.

Young Man 8 I do I do I do I do I do!!

Young Man 2 and Young Man 8 kiss.

Morgan Are all of you married?

Tristan Find me a man who is worth a damn and I will marry the son of a bitch.

Morgan What about Jasper?

Jasper Jasper is not the marrying kind.

Morgan Why not?

Young Man 6 Jasper dates young guys.

Young Man 4 Like, just out of college young?

Jasper Jasper doesn't like complicated men.

Morgan Are Eric and Toby married?

Young Man 1 Not yet.

Young Man 3 I have a question.

Morgan Yes?

Young Man 3 How can Eric afford such a nice apartment?

Young Man 7 Yeah, I was wondering that too.

Morgan In order to understand who Eric Glass is, one first has to understand the significance of his family's apartment on the Upper West Side.

Young Man 1 Eric's grandfather, Nathan, was a veteran of the 10th Armored Division, which helped liberate Dachau. His grandmother, Miriam, a refugee from Germany.

Morgan In the fall of 1947, they signed the lease on a rent-controlled apartment on West End Avenue. This was back when middle-class families could afford such places.

Eric This apartment became the first place Eric's grandmother felt safe in the world. She raised her family here in this apartment. Voted in every election at the public school around the corner. She watched John Kennedy's death, Richard Nixon's resignation, and Barack Obama's election from the living room of this apartment. It was in this apartment that Miriam Glass became an American.

Young Man 1 After her death in December 2008, Eric took up residence in the apartment in order to continue the family's claim on the cherished dwelling. He met Toby Darling a week later.

Toby Toby Darling entered Eric's life like a typhoon.

Young Man 1 The two instantly fell in love and Toby moved in four months later.

Eric For Eric, it was everything he'd ever wanted in a relationship.

Toby For Toby, it was . . .

Morgan For Toby, it was a home that was safe and stable and loving.

Young Man 1 Toby inspired Eric. Eric protected Toby.

Toby Toby fucked the living daylights out of Eric.

Eric Eric and Toby had really great sex.

Morgan Thank you, gentlemen. Now that we know what Eric cares about most, we must give him something to fight against. A few days before Christmas that year, Eric receives a call from his father informing him that the building's management company has finally decided to begin eviction proceedings against the Glass family.

Eric No, please not that.

Young Man 1 They're hiring a lawyer and planning to fight it.

Morgan But it is possible that 2016 could be Eric's last year living in his family's cherished home.

Eric Not my home, my grandparents' home.

Morgan What would Eric do after receiving such news?

Eric He would want to be comforted by Toby.

Morgan Is Toby particularly good at providing comfort?

Eric Well . . .

Young Man 1 No.

Morgan So what could Toby do that would make Eric feel better right now?

Young Man 1 He could fuck the living daylights out of Eric.

Eric Toby is very good at that.

Morgan Yes, but so soon in the story?

The Lads insist: definitely, yes.

If that's what you need.

End of Scene Two.

SCENE THREE

December, 2015

1. Eric and Toby's Apartment

Toby God, if I'd known playwriting was this hard, I'd have turned my book into a TV show instead. I spent the entire day writing the same speech over and over. But I think it's good. Would you read it for me?

Eric Yes, of course, I'd love to. But later. I thought we could do something else in the meantime.

Toby Wait, are you naked?

Eric Why don't you join me and find out?

Toby What about dinner?

Eric We can order in.

Toby Yeah but if we wait too long it'll take forever and you know I have to eat by eight / or I won't be able to sleep . . .

Eric Remember that time you told me to meet you at the Whitney in the tightest jeans I owned and no underwear?

Toby I miss the old Whitney.

Eric It was a John Currin exhibition and you kept trying to slide your hands down inside my jeans.

Toby The new one is so far *away*.

Eric My jeans were so tight you couldn't even get your hand in. But you huffed and you puffed and then finally you got your hand down in there.

Toby But I do like the views upstairs.

Eric And then you couldn't get it out.

Toby You were the one who decided to do squats all week.

Eric Oh I *do* have your attention.

Toby You definitely had my attention in those jeans.

Eric I've spent a lot of time at the squat rack this week.

Morgan Toby undresses, and joins Eric in bed.

Toby Get over here. That ass needs a face in it.

Toby God, I love your ass. How does a Jewish boy from Westchester end up with an ass this nice? Must be from your mother's side of the family.

Eric Can we not talk about my mother while I have an erection?

Toby You have an erection? I want an erection. How come he has an erection and I don't?

Eric Here . . .

Young Man 1 Eric dives under the covers and starts blowing him.

Toby Okay! Get me hard, baby.
   Oh wow.
   Oh yeah.
   Oh fuck, baby, yeah.
   It's not working.

Eric Think of something sexy.

Toby Remember that time on Fire Island when we watched those two guys fucking in the Meat Rack? That was so hot.

Eric That's working.

Toby Yeah. I wish we'd done that. You riding my cock on a sheet in the Meat Rack. Oh yeah, there we go.

Eric Fuck me, Toby.

Toby Yeah, you want me to fuck you?

Eric I just said that I did.

Toby Right. I was just going along with, I . . . right, I'll fuck you like we're in the Meat Rack.

Eric What is with you and the Meat Rack all of a sudden? That was like / five years ago.

Toby I don't know, I thought it was hot, didn't you?

Eric Yeah, but I haven't been obsessing on it ever since.

Toby I wouldn't say I was obsessing. It just popped into my mind just now is all.

Eric Toby, slide your dick inside me right now.

Toby Yes sir!

Morgan Toby starts to enter Eric.

Toby That okay?

Eric Hold on . . .
   Okay, try again.
   Slowly.
   No. Wrong angle.
   That's . . . not even close.

Toby Well did it move?

Eric Same place it's always been.

Toby How's that?

Eric There you go. Slowly.

Toby More?

Eric A little.

Morgan Toby slides in more.

Toby Fuck, that feels good.

Eric Okay, more.

Toby 'More' is the rest.

Eric Yeah, go for it.

Morgan Toby slides in all the way. They both moan, feeling good. They fuck slowly.

Toby Wow, you're tight. When was the last time you –

Eric What?

Toby Did you . . . you know . . . hook up with anyone when I took that trip to Chicago last month?

Eric Why? Did you?

Toby This one boy on Grindr.

Eric How was he?

Toby Kinda hot actually. What about you?

Eric Last for me was this guy last fall. I forget where you were.

Toby How was he?

Eric Eh. He fucked me like he was doing me a favor.

Morgan They fuck *silently*.

After a moment:

Toby Should we order Chinese tonight?

Eric We had Chinese last night.

Toby You like Chinese.

Eric Toby, I don't know. Can we talk about this after?

Toby It's just that I'd like to know what we're ordering when we're done so we can get right on it.

Eric Get on my ass, motherfucker.

Toby Yeah, you want my dick, little boy?

Eric Toby, ew.

Toby Sorry.

Morgan Eric gets on top of Toby and starts to ride him.

Eric Fuck me, Toby.

Toby Like that?

Eric Harder.

Toby Like that?

Eric Harder.

Toby I can't really go any / harder.

Eric Fuck me harder.

Toby That feel good?

Eric That feels amazing. I love you, Toby.

Toby Oh God, I'm close already. Shit, I'm sorry.

Eric It's okay, Toby. Come inside me.
Yeah, Toby. Yeah.
God I love you.
I love you.
I love you.
God, I wanna get married.

Toby What?

Eric Oh fuck, nothing. Forget I said that.

Toby You wanna get married?

Eric Bad timing, bad timing. Keep going.

Toby But now it's just out there.

Eric Forget I said anything. Just bring it home, baby.

Toby Okay.

Morgan Toby starts to bring it home.

Toby Are you thinking like a big fancy wedding?

Eric We don't have to talk about this now.

Toby Oh fuck, I'm getting close.
Oh God.

Eric Yeah.

Toby Oh God.

Eric Yeah.

Toby Oh God.

Eric Yeah.

Morgan Release the hounds!

Toby Oh God!!
Fuck, that was good.

They lay there a moment.

You wanna get married?

Eric Forget it.

Toby No, Eric . . . tell me.

Eric Yes, Toby. I do. I have for a while.

Toby Why didn't you say something before?

Eric Just waiting for the right moment, I guess.

A beat, then:

You don't have to answer right away. But I would like to talk about it. I mean, we've been together seven years and I do want to spend the rest / of my –

Toby Yeah, fuck it, why not?

Eric We can talk about it another time.

Toby I think we should do it. Should we have the party here?

Eric Oh. Well. Actually –

Toby Yeah, you're right: we'll save up for a really nice wedding. Maybe at the Plaza or in Maui.

Eric That's really expensive, babe. It's not like I make a fortune / and –

Toby We'll be able to afford it. Gimme a year. Two at the most. I'm going to finish this play and it's going to get produced and I will finally show people that I'm worthy of their attention. And their respect. And eventually their money. And we will build something real for ourselves, not just borrowed. Something that's ours. How's that sound?

Eric is a little amazed at his certainty.

Eric Uh, yeah. Let's do that.

Toby Deal.

Eric So, did we just get engaged?

Toby I think we just did.

Eric Holy shit! I've got your cum inside my ass and we just got engaged.

Toby Where's *that* Cole Porter song?

Eric I love you, Toby.

2. Toby Interlude

Morgan Yes, well done. Now: why didn't Eric tell Toby about the apartment? Why did he choose to seduce him rather than inform him?

Eric It isn't a certainty yet. And Toby is so focused on writing his play.

Morgan I think there's another reason. One that touches on Toby's nature – perhaps even Toby's past. I think we must take a moment to examine the deep truths of Toby's soul. Let's start with his writing, for it seems to be driving his character.

Young Man 1 Toby has written a novel based on his childhood.

Morgan Excellent. Now, if I may: the book is good, not great. It's engaging, and wittily written. If a touch facile.

Young Man 1 It's published as a young adult novel.

Morgan What's the name of Toby's central character?

Young Man 1 Elan.

Morgan Perfect.

Toby Rich kid, seventeen, raised on the Upper West Side, sexy as fuck, sarcastic, rude, yet undeniably compelling. He's basically me.

Morgan Or.
  Elan is everything Toby has ever wanted to be. He is who Toby has convinced himself – and the world – that he's become.

Toby Are you saying that Toby's life is a lie?

Morgan I'm saying that the truth is something he has spent his life running from.

Toby That doesn't sound very fun.

Morgan It isn't.
  Springtime. New York City Ballet. A rainstorm.

End of Scene Three.

SCENE FOUR

Spring and Summer 2016

1. Lincoln Center

A heavy rainstorm. Toby stands under the massive eaves, smoking a cigarette and dressed in a very smart suit. A large, expensive umbrella in his hand.

Young Man 1 emerges from the lobby, sees the rain and rifles through his bag for an umbrella, finding none. He then looks over and notices Toby.

Young Man 1 Toby? You're Toby, right? Toby Darling?

Toby Hey, thanks for reading. I'm sorry I don't have a pen on me.

Young Man 1 No, I . . . we met maybe six months ago. At your apartment? We had each other's bags.

Toby Oh yeah. The little kleptomaniac.

Young Man 1 Hey, you took *my* bag. I'm Adam Lucas McDowell.

Toby Oh, the full name, wow. In that case, I'm Toby Michael Darling.

Adam What a small world.

Toby The world is big. Manhattan is small.

Adam Yeah, I guess so. You look . . . wow.

Toby Aw, thanks. I was going for 'wow'. You usually dress like that for the ballet?

Adam Oh. No, I . . . I grabbed a rush ticket spur of the moment. Is your boyfriend with you?

Toby Eric ended up working late tonight. Beautiful second-tier seat gone to waste.

Adam I was all the way in the back.

Toby Well, someone has to be. What'd you think?

Adam Oh, of the program? Really good. I loved the new piece most especially.

Toby Yeah. Life-changing, in fact.

Adam Oh! Speaking of life-changing, I read your book.

Toby Get out.

Adam I really loved it. So vivid, so fully realized. Like Salinger, almost.

Toby 'Almost'? What do you mean / 'almost'?

Adam Oh. I just mean, you know, Salinger's one of the greatest American writers / of all time and –

Toby I'm just fucking with you.

Adam The character of Elan is so vibrant. He pops, you know? I know that kid. I grew up with that kid.

Toby The snobby gay rich kid?

Adam He's not snobby, he's just particular.

Toby That's what I always say!

Adam Well I loved it. And I'm glad I got a chance to tell you.

The rain intensifies.

Toby Do you have an umbrella?

Adam I thought I did.

Toby I can walk you to the train.

Adam I actually live not too far from here.

Morgan Do you? Where?

Adam Oh, um. Over on 74th Street?

Toby And what?

Adam Riverside?

Toby What, like with a dozen roommates or something?

Adam No, I . . . I live with my parents.

Toby Oh . . .

Adam Yeah, so.
    I don't mind / walking in the rain.

Toby Nonsense. It's pouring out. You'll catch your death.

Morgan They huddled together under Toby's umbrella
and headed out into the monsoon. Eventually they
arrived at Adam's apartment, which was . . .

Young Man 1 Oh. A five-bedroom, six-and-a-half-
bathroom with park and river views that took up half of
the eleventh floor of a majestic neo-Georgian building.
For you see: Adam Lucas McDowell was filthy stinkin'
rich.

2. Adam's Apartment

Toby Oh wow.

Adam You can come in if you want.

Toby I don't want to bother your parents.

Adam They're in Japan right now. My dad has scotch,
if you want. Like really old scotch.

Toby How old is 'really old'? Like from the Clinton
administration?

Adam No, like from the Treaty of Versailles.

Toby Um, yeah, I'll have a glass.

Adam pours Toby's drink.

This place is amazing.

Adam It's just my home, no biggie.
Here you go.

Toby sips.

Toby Dear God.

Adam Is it okay?

Toby Baby, you've just handed me the last century of world history distilled into spirit form. It's a quintillion times better than okay.

Morgan Toby moved over to the massive bookcase. There on the shelf – in front of what looked like a priceless first edition of *The Great Gatsby* – was a photograph of Adam with the President and his wife, taken inside that very room.

Toby Toby sipped the scotch, knowing that each swallow was worth more than what he currently had in his checking account. Toby felt his sense of status plummeting. (*To Adam.*) How do you know the Obamas?

Adam My mom went to law school with him. It broke her heart when I decided to go to Yale.

Toby Yes, I'm sure that's every mother's nightmare.

Adam Did you go to grad school for writing?

Toby I didn't study writing in grad school.

Morgan A clever dodge, a linguistic sleight of hand: Toby hadn't even finished high school.

Toby What did you study?

Adam English.

Toby How daring.

Adam Yeah, I know.

Toby And now you're . . . ?

Adam An actor.

Toby Of course you are.

Adam Where did you go / to school?

Toby Any luck so far? With the acting?

Adam I get called back a lot. Haven't booked a real job yet, but there are a few agents and managers I've been talking to.

Toby Not bad for your first year.

Adam I've got friends on Broadway already.

Toby And I'm sure you're just sooooo happy for them.

Adam I am.

Toby I believe you.

Adam No, I am. It's just, you know . . .

Toby 'When's it gonna be my turn?'

Adam Yeah.

Toby Believe me I understand that feeling.

Adam It's like such a struggle sometimes.

Toby What the fuck do you know about struggle, rich boy? Some of us had to work our asses off to become the mediocrities that we are today. Brave choice, rich boy. Go be an artist. You're the only ones who can afford to anymore.

Morgan But what Toby actually said was:

Toby Don't give up, Adam. Keep struggling. It'll be worth it in the end.

Adam Thank you. It's exciting that you're adapting your book for theatre. Do you know what's happening with it?

Toby Actually I do. My agent's good friends with the director Tom Durrell. Do you know him?

Adam No, should I?

Toby Yes, you absolutely should. He's a genius. Anyway, Tom read my play and really flipped for it. We've been developing it and workshopping it all winter long and we go into production in Chicago this September.

Adam What does Elan look like? You don't give a lot of physical details in the book. Is that on purpose?

Toby So every boy who reads it can believe that they're him.

Adam That's exactly the experience I had! I'm convinced he looks like me.

Toby Maybe he does.

Morgan It's stopped raining.

Toby I should go.

Adam Would you sign my copy first?

Toby Yeah, of course.

He inscribes Adam's book.

Morgan 'To Adam, whom I hope to be when I grow up.'

Adam Thank you.

Toby Hey, how'd you like to come have dinner at our place next week?

Adam Really? Yeah, I'd love that!

Toby Great. I know Eric would love to see you again.

Morgan Toby left, forgetting his umbrella. Adam picked it up and saw its condition. It had all gone along the seams and been re-patched. In truth, it was an appalling umbrella. But from a distance it was dazzling. Like its owner, it did not bear close scrutiny.

Morgan As he rode the wood-paneled elevator down to the lobby, Toby thought . . .

Toby Who the fuck is that kid? Boy, did he bury the lede that first time we met him.

Morgan What was he going to say? 'Hi, I'm Adam and I'm a child of privilege'?

Toby Yes! I'd have cards printed up, I'd have T-shirts made!

Morgan Oh Toby.
  So now we have Eric, we have Toby, and we have Adam. Time to bring all three together.

Young Man 1 A week later, Adam walked twenty blocks north and joined Eric and Toby for dinner.

3. Eric and Toby's Apartment

Eric What do you *mean*. you've never seen a Truffaut film?

Toby Okay, calm down. He's only twenty-one. / What does he know?

Eric But he grew up in Manhattan!

Adam My parents aren't really into movies. We did see a Broadway show every Thanksgiving.

Eric Okay, so let's start there. What's your favorite play of all time?

Adam *Mamma Mia!*

Eric Let's start with movies instead. Can we assume that if it's in black and white you haven't seen it?

Adam Yes.

Eric Great. We should start with the French New Wave and then mix in American seventies cinema. *400 Blows*.

Toby Not a movie about blowjobs.

Eric *Jules et Jim.*

Toby Not a movie about homos. *Bonnie and Clyde*.

Eric *The Conversation*. Then there are the contemporary classics. We should show him *Beau Travail*!

Toby Oh God. Do not show him fucking *Beau Travail*. Run, Adam. Save yourself.

Eric Better yet: what's something you've never seen that you've always been curious about? There's no wrong answer.

Adam Well. I've always wanted to see *The Deer Hunter*.

Eric and Toby look at each other.

Eric Oh. *The Deer Hunter*.

Toby I mean, it's a classic.

Eric Great cast.

Toby Epic sweep.

Eric Meryl Streep.

Toby Eric . . .

Toby It's just a little, well . . .

Eric ⎤ Heavy.
Toby ⎦ Long.

Adam Oh. Yeah, that's okay. Whatever you think is best.

Beat.

Eric You know what? Fuck it. Let's watch *The Deer Hunter.*

Adam No, we don't have to / watch it tonight.

Eric When broadening our horizons, the word 'no' is not in our vocabulary.

Toby Unless Eric thinks your taste is for shit.

Morgan And so they watched *The Deer Hunter*. Adam returned the next night for –

Young Man 7 *Breathless.*

Morgan And then the next night for –

Young Man 2 *Jules et Jim.*

Morgan Eric and Toby took Adam under their wings that spring and early summer, folding him into their lives as if he had always been there. Adam found himself at Eric and Toby's with increasing frequency, even going so far as to leave some clothes in their guest bedroom.

Young Man 1 A fondness and an intimacy grew between them – a kind that Adam had never experienced before with older gay men.

Eric Older?!

Toby Fuck you, kid!

Young Man 1 It was, in fact, the first adult friendship of Adam's life.

Morgan Eric delighted in filling in the gaps in Adam's cultural education, making regular visits with him to –

Young Man 5 Film Forum –

Young Man 6 – and MOMA.

Young Man 8 They visited the Delacorte –

Young Man 3 – went for day trips to Jacob Riis Beach –

Young Man 4 – and hiking in Bear Mountain.

Toby Really, hiking?

Adam I loved it.

Morgan Eric taught Adam how to cook and introduced him to his favorite writers.

Toby Toby participated in these events but not as often and always at a remove. He spent most of that summer feverishly rewriting his play.

4. *Adam and Eric*

Adam I want to ask you something because I don't know how to ask Toby.

Eric Okay . . .

Adam Do you think Toby would let me audition for his play?

Eric You should ask him!

Adam I was hoping you'd ask him for me. I don't feel as close to Toby as I do to you. Or, what I mean to say is: I'm not sure how Toby feels about me.

Eric Toby adores you.

Adam He's sometimes cold and cutting.

Eric Oh Adam. Toby doesn't pet with gentle hands, it's true. But I do know he's very fond of you.

Adam Still, would you talk to him for me?

5. *Eric and Toby*

Toby Waste of time.

Eric How much time could it possibly take? It's one audition.

Toby He isn't even a trained actor. He's got a BA in blowjobs from Yale.

Eric If he's not right, you send him home, that's the end of it. Would you at least talk to him?

6. *Toby and Adam*

Toby First of all, next time you want a favor from me, you ask me and not Eric, okay?

Adam I didn't want to bother you.

Toby Second of all, you're not going to get far in this business if you're afraid of bothering people. Now, do you want to audition for my play?

Adam Yes.

Toby Why?

Adam It's a great part.

Toby No shit. Is that the only reason?

Adam I want to prove myself to you.

Toby Me? Why me?

Adam Because I admire you, Toby.

Toby is completely taken aback, then regroups.

Toby The role is Everest.

Young Man 3 Oh boy.

Toby Elan never leaves the stage the entire play. He has more lines than Hamlet.

Young Man 7 Really, Toby? Hamlet?

Toby Shut up. (*To Adam.*) Think you're up to it?

Adam Yes.

Toby Okay, then. But you'd better prepare. I'm not going to go to bat for you just to have you shit the bed once you get inside the room.

7. *Toby and Eric*

Morgan And so Adam auditioned for Toby's play and, to Toby's great astonishment, it was as if Adam became Elan right there in the room.

Toby Jesus –

Eric So is he going to get the part?

Toby He has to go through callbacks. But so far he's everyone's favorite. That kid is really special, Eric.

Eric Yeah, babe. I've been telling you that for weeks now.

Toby I mean as an actor. Or at least as this character. It's kind of perfect, when you think about it.

Eric How do you mean?

Toby Well, Adam's this spoiled little rich kid.

Eric Adam isn't spoiled.

Toby I just mean they've had similar upbringings.

Eric They're very different people, Toby.

Toby What do you know? Elan is my character.

Eric And Adam's my friend.

Toby He's my friend, too.

Eric So be nicer to him.

Toby I may be giving him his first professional job, for Chrissake. How much nicer can I be? Let's just pray he doesn't fuck it up.

8. Eric and Adam

Adam When did you know Toby was the man you wanted to marry?

Eric Well, I think if I was honest, I'd say it was the night I first met him. The following seven years was basically due diligence. But remember: when Toby and I met – and certainly when we were growing up – marriage wasn't an option for us. I just knew he was someone I could spend my life with. Are you thinking about proposing to someone?

Adam No. I'm just curious about your relationship. Who proposed to who?

Morgan Eric proposed to Toby.

Adam Did you get down on one knee?

Eric I was kind of on both knees at the time.

Adam Are you and Toby going to have children?

Eric I'd love to have children. I've always dreamed of it.

Morgan But of course, Toby had a difficult childhood.

Toby What?

Eric I don't even know the whole story.

Morgan Toby's parents died when he was young.

Toby Morgan.

Adam I didn't know that.

Eric I only really know the contours of Toby's story.

Morgan He moved to New York when he was seventeen.

Toby Hold on.

Adam I thought he was raised in New York.

Eric That's a complicated history.

Toby Please stop.

Eric He doesn't talk about his past – not even to me.

Adam Does that bother you?

Eric It used to. But Toby has let me know him in ways he won't let others. I've learned to understand what love looks like to him.

Adam What does love look like to *you*?

Eric Taking care of Toby, I guess. Because no one ever has.

Adam Do you and Toby still have sex?

Morgan Yes, they do.

Eric We do okay.

Adam Do you . . . ever have sex with other people?

Eric Let's just say there's a difference between monogamy and monotony.

Adam Would you and Toby ever want to have sex with me?

Toby Say yes.

Eric Oh.

Adam I'm sorry.

Toby Say yes.

Eric No. no, don't be sorry.

Toby Just say yes, we'll figure out the details later.

Eric That is a very flattering and tempting offer.

Toby And so . . .

Adam You don't / have to –

Eric No, truly. You're very attractive.

Toby He's hot as fuck.

Eric And under different circumstances I would be all over that.

Toby Yeah, baby.

Eric Or under that.

Toby Yeah, baby.

Eric Whichever you prefer.

Toby Yeah, baby!

Eric But here's why I think it might not be a good idea: if you were to get the job in Toby's play, I think you don't want that energy between you as you work.

Toby What?!

Eric And if you don't get that job . . . well, maybe this friendship is about something different. In other words: let's not go and fuck up a good thing.

Toby You're killing me, Eric.

Adam Yes. Yes, you're right. I'm sorry.

Eric Do not apologize.

Adam I don't really know what I'm doing.

Eric You seem to be doing just fine.

Adam Could I . . . keep talking to you? Like, could I sometimes . . . come to you for direction? Advice? For wisdom?

Eric You want wisdom . . . from me?

Adam Yes. Very much.

Eric Oh. Well.

Morgan How about a little perspective instead?

Eric For whatever that's worth.

Adam Yes. Perspective. I'd love that. Thank you, Eric.

Morgan Eric had never been solicited both for sex and for wisdom in the same conversation. For all of his life, he'd been someone's son, younger brother, or student. There had always been someone in front of him to look up to. It had never occurred to him that eventually there'd be someone behind him, looking up to him.

Eric Adam's request made Eric feel valued – perhaps even important – in a way he had never felt before.

Young Man 3 I'm sorry – can I ask another question?

Morgan Of course.

Young Man 3 Earlier you said Eric wasn't special. Do you really think that's true?

Young Man 1 Morgan said Eric didn't *think* he was special.

Young Man 3 But how can he possibly think that? He seems pretty remarkable to me.

Morgan You've just stumbled across a great secret that not even Eric knows. Eric Glass was wrong about himself in every imaginable way. Not only was he the bravest person he knew, he also possessed the ability to change the world to an extent far greater than Toby or any of the countless brilliant people with whom he surrounded himself. Eric Glass's entire conception of himself was false. He simply didn't know it yet.

Eric How will he learn?

Morgan Heartbreak.

9. *Eric, Toby and Adam*

Morgan So: does Adam get the job?

The Lads really want him to. All eyes on Toby.

Toby Yeah, fuck it. Let's give him the job.

The Lads celebrate.

Adam I can't believe this is happening!

Toby I can. You worked your ass off for this.

Eric Congratulations, Adam.

Adam I really want to do an amazing job for you, Toby.

Toby You'd fucking better, kid.

Adam I will, I promise. Oh shit, this is real, isn't it? I'm going to be playing this part. Who else is going to be in it? I have some friends I could recommend for the ensemble. Do you know where your apartment is going to be in Chicago? Maybe we can take yoga classes together. I'm going to be off book from day one.

Morgan Toby led Adam out onto the terrace and before Eric could join them, the door closed, creating a separation between them. Eric watched on the other side of the plate glass window as Toby and Adam hugged and laughed and daydreamed together.

End of Scene Four.

Autumn 2016

Young Man 7 Toby and Adam left for Chicago after Labor Day, leaving Eric by himself.

Young Man 8 Eric almost instantly became lonely.

Young Man 4 For the first time in years, his beloved home was quiet.

Young Man 1 And then one morning, a chance encounter with an old friend upended not just his silence, but also his life.

Young Man 4 The reunion occurred, of all places, on Eric's elevator.

Eric Walter? My goodness, hello.

Walter Eric Glass?

Eric Are you visiting someone in the building?

Walter No, Henry and I are subletting for a few months while our new place is being renovated.

Eric Stop. Toby and I live on the fifteenth floor.

Walter Imagine that.

The elevator dings as they arrive in the lobby.

Eric Listen, Walter: I feel really bad about ghosting on you like I did last year.

Walter 'Ghosting'?

Eric Falling off the face of the earth after . . . well, you know . . .

Walter I told you to put that out of your mind.

Eric Yes I know you did but . . . well, I wasn't sure if you'd put it out of *yours*. And so I just . . . well, I didn't handle it well. And I'm sorry.

Walter Apology accepted. Now / if you don't mind –

Eric I'd love to invite you and Henry over for dinner one night.

Walter Henry's in London through Thanksgiving.

Eric Oh. Toby's in Chicago. I guess we're both on our own this autumn.

Walter Yes, it seems we are.

Young Man 2 A week later, Eric slipped a note under Walter's door:

Eric 'Walter, if you're up for it, I'd love to invite you over for dinner tomorrow. Stop by around seven if you'd like. Apartment 15A. Eric.'

Young Man 3 The doorbell rang at seven sharp.

Eric Please, come in.

Young Man 6 There was a frailty to Walter that was new.

Young Man 2 What had once been a distant, inscrutable aspect was now positively spectral.

Young Man 4 Eric instinctively put his hand on Walter's back as if to steady him as he passed. The older man shrugged off the gesture without a word.

Eric Eric could feel how thin Walter was, the bones of his vertebrae reaching out to meet Eric's hand in that brief moment of connection. (*Then:*) You know, I think this is the first time you and I have ever been alone together.

Walter That can't be true.

Eric I think it is. What if we discover that Henry and Toby are the interesting ones and that you and I actually have nothing to say to each other?

Walter That's what alcohol is for.

Eric Would you like a glass of wine?

Walter I'm fine, thank you. Your apartment is enormous.

Eric Oh, yes. How long have you and Henry been together?

Walter Oh. Over thirty-six years.

Eric That's amazing.

Walter There isn't all that much to it, really. Just a succession of dinners.

Eric I wish I knew Henry better.

Walter After thirty-six years I don't feel I completely know him.

Eric I feel the same way about Toby. Oh! Toby and I are getting married next year.

Walter Really? Congratulations.

Eric Thank you.

Walter I've always had the impression that you and Toby were ill-matched.

Eric Oh.

Walter That came out wrong.

Eric There's a right way to say that?

Walter I'm sure there is.
  Yes: opposites attract.

Eric Ah.

Walter Some relationships thrive on tension.

Eric I wouldn't say we were always in tension.

Walter Opposition maybe.

Eric I think we get along just fine.

Walter You know, I think I will have some wine after all.

Eric pours two glasses of wine.

How big *is* your apartment?

Eric Three bedrooms, two baths. All the other units in the building have been divided and subdivided over the years, turned into condos. This is the only rental unit left in the building.

Walter You rent this apartment?

Eric God yes, I couldn't afford to own this. It's rent-controlled. I only pay five hundred and seventy-five dollars a month for all of this.

Young Man 2 What?!

Young Man 6 Five hundred and seventy-five dollars!

Young Man 8 Fuck you.

Young Man 4 I mean, Jesus!

Eric My father took his first steps right over there. My mother was sitting in that very chair you're in when my father proposed to her. I don't think I've spent a Thanksgiving or a Passover anywhere else.

Walter I envy you that.

Eric Don't. Our Seders are endless.

Walter No, I mean the connection to your family's history through your family's home. To live in the same place your father was raised – that's pretty remarkable, Eric. It must inform so much of your life.

Eric grows quiet.

Walter I said something wrong again, didn't I?

Eric No. The truth is I'm probably going to be evicted at the end of the year.

Walter Evicted? Oh. I'm sorry. On what grounds?

Eric The lease is ironclad. If my grandmother isn't in residence for more than a year, they can call the whole thing off.

Walter Where does she live now?

Eric In that urn on the mantle just behind you.
    I mean, technically she's still in residence but I don't think they see it that way.
    My parents are fighting it, but . . . things aren't looking good. If I look on the bright side, I think it might be exciting to start a new chapter in my life. But it won't be this place and it won't have this history.

Walter At least you'll have Toby.

Eric I decided to befriend you and Henry because I thought: 'That's going to be me and Toby someday. I'd better study how they did it.'

Walter Yes, I suspected as much. The truth is I'm bad at new relationships. Henry travels so much. We're always in a new city, and never long enough to put down roots.

Eric That must be hard.

Walter Part of the bargain.

Eric You think of your relationship as a 'bargain'? I'm sorry. That was rude. Don't answer that.

Walter Every relationship in Henry's life is a kind of bargain. Henry is a businessman and therefore sees the world exclusively in those terms. He cares most about the things he can use. Money, supremely useful. Intellect, fairly useful. People, intermittently useful. Sentiment,

not the least bit useful. I do not subscribe to this view.
But that is who Henry is.

Eric And who are you?

Walter Me?

I'm the man who fell in love with Henry Wilcox.

Henry was born in Ohio, in the late 1950s. He was a
star of track and field. First in his class and president of
the student body association. As American as an Aaron
Copland symphony. He married Patricia Fitzgerald while
still in college. Two sons arrived soon after and Henry
was on his way to a life of success and diligence and
robust Episcopalianism. And if strapping, ascendant
young men with bright futures and beautiful families had
secret desires and shameful urges, they hid them from the
world, from themselves. Henry worked hard, kept his
head down and his hands to himself. Eventually his hard
work led him out of the Midwest and into the heart of
American business as well as the heart of American
temptation: New York City. The Wilcox family arrived
on July 3, 1981. The same summer that I arrived.

Like so many before me, I arrived in New York a
refugee from a home that had grown hostile to my
presence. I was aware from an early age that I made
people uncomfortable. I was moony and effeminate. But
small towns have the peculiar habit of tolerating their
feathery, delicate boys – provided they are born to wealthy
and (needless to say) white families. Once I grew older,
my parents sent me to ministers, to psychiatrists, to
fitness instructors even. Every walk through town felt
dangerous, every school day possessed the potential for
violence. I would steal my mother's sleeping pills, hoarding
them, planning my suicide. I would stare at them nightly,
holding them in my hands, telling myself they were the
pathway out of my pain, that they would heal me more
effectively than any psychiatrist, that they were more
powerful than prayer. I stared and stared at them until

one night, perilously close to swallowing them, I was struck by the realization that I didn't want to change, and that what I hated was not my nature, but rather my circumstances. And so I left . . . to seek not my fame and certainly not my fortune, but rather – and rather simply – my dignity.

The only place I knew to go was New York. I had read about the events of June 1969. It was the only place in the world I knew to look for young men like me.

Imagine me at nineteen years old in the middle of Times Square in 1981 – 120 pounds and skin so pale it was practically translucent, my mother's old Samsonite suitcase in my hands, asking strangers for directions to the Stonewall Inn.

Eventually I was given directions by a very friendly pimp.

I rode the graffiti-covered subway downtown, gripping my suitcase so tightly that blisters formed on my hands. I made my way to the fabled Stonewall Inn only to discover that it has become . . . a Chinese Restaurant.

You can imagine my disappointment.

But I was very hungry. And I'd never eaten Chinese food before. So I stayed in Mr Shun's Dim Sum Emporium and I knew that I had made the right decision.

Henry, meanwhile, is not so certain. He's twenty-four and already the father of two young boys, earning more money in a month than most men twice his age make in a year. He owns a four-bedroom house in White Plains and he commutes daily to his office downtown. There's Henry, knocking back after-work martinis with his colleagues. There's Henry in the steam room at the East Side Club. There's Henry on the 11:30 train headed home to his family. There's Henry in the shower, remorseful and penitent, attempting to expunge his great secret from his skin. There's Henry sliding into bed at one in the morning next to a wife who suspects more than she lets on.

We meet at a rooftop party overlooking Christopher Street. Henry's rented an apartment in the city while his family spends its summer on Cape Cod. I notice him first and am thunderstruck by the sight of him. Honey chestnut hair worn slightly long as was the style of the day. Well-developed chest threatening the integrity of the polo shirt he's wearing. I move into his line of sight and wait to be noticed. It doesn't take long. We chat for as long as we can stand to, then head back to his apartment and his bed.

Henry was the first, the only man I ever loved. No, that's a blatant lie and shame on me for telling it. Henry Wilcox was the only man I ever needed to be loved by. It was in Henry's gaze, from his kisses and through his touch that I finally glimpsed my own worth. I fell hard into Henry's handsomeness, his intelligence, his potential . . . no, not his potential . . . his certainty.

I was never meant to be Henry's life partner. I was the person he was dancing with when the music stopped. By that point, whispers of disease had graduated to rumors. Rumors became stories. And stories became fact. Henry had arrived at the party just in time for it to end.

For five years, Henry and I clung to one other for safety, for comfort, as the city burned around us. By the summer of 1987, we had had enough of funerals and hospital visits and the sight of once-vital men laid to waste. We looked for a house as far from civilization as we could find. We finally stumbled across a rambling old farmhouse on an aimless country road, three hours north of here, built in the late eighteenth century. It's set off from the road so you have the illusion of being alone in the world. And in front of the house, my favorite thing on the property: an enormous cherry tree that has been there since the time George Washington was out terrorizing them. It puts on the most astonishing show twice a year. In the autumn, it burns deep orange and red leaves, as if the tree were on fire. And in the spring, vibrant blushing flowers which eventually fall ever so gently to the ground in a kind of aerial ballet.

Walter becomes caught in his reverie. Eventually:

And – I don't know if you'll believe me but it's true – deep in the trunk of the tree are a set of pig's teeth that were put there I don't know how many generations ago. The superstition among the colonials was that if you bite the bark of the tree, it will cure all your ailments.

Eric Does it?

Walter No. Of course it doesn't. Pure superstition. And yet, there in the country, on rolling pastureland, with flowers and breezes and cherry trees with pig's teeth stuck in the bark, there was no death, there was no illness, there was no loss or danger. Henry bought it the next day and we lived there for a year without ever leaving the area. We cooked, we gardened, we read underneath the cherry tree. And we avoided all news from our friends, from the outside world.

After a year, Henry grew restless. He began traveling to London to start the first of his many ventures that would eventually make him a very wealthy man. Without him, I began to stew – and so early one morning I decided to return to the city. I hadn't been there in over a year. I was about to take myself to lunch when I ran into an old friend of ours. Peter West was his name. Dear Peter. Darling man, more clever than anyone I ever knew. And handsome as sin. I wouldn't have recognized him if he hadn't called out to me from across Fifth Avenue. Peter had 'the look', the telltale sign that someone was infected. His handsome face was sunken and sallow, his muscles had melted away. He was also, I discovered, essentially homeless. His landlord evicted him. He'd been estranged from his family for years. He had nowhere to go. We took the next train upstate and phoned for a cab.

The driver took one look at Peter and fled. We stood there, four miles from my house with no other means to get there but our legs. The day was beautiful and Peter smiled as he breathed in the country air through his rattling lungs. The sun was setting as we approached the house. I could feel a release in Peter's body. I put him in one of the rooms upstairs. Peter spent the next five days slowly dying. I cleaned him when he fouled himself. I held him as he wept in grief. I comforted him as he screamed in pain. I had no idea I had such strength. On Peter's fourth day, Henry returned from London. When I told him that Peter was upstairs, Henry flew into a rage, accusing me of betrayal, of bringing the plague into our home. I had never seen such fear on a man's face as I saw in Henry's that day. He got back into his car and drove away. Peter died as the sun was rising his fifth day with us. Henry returned to London, leaving me alone for several months without so much as a phone call. I spent the first few weeks of my exile wondering if I was wrong to show such kindness to a friend. But, oh Eric, to see Peter's ravaged face, and to look into those frightened eyes, I believe that if I had left Peter on that sidewalk, returning to my place of peace without him, I would have ruined that house for myself far more than I ever could have ruined it for Henry. I eventually came to see that leaving the city and our friends behind was as unforgivable an act of cowardice as I have ever performed. The answer, I realized, was not to shut the world out but rather to fling the doors open and to invite it in. And so, while Henry's furious silence roared at me from across the Atlantic, I brought others in their last days up to the house. I replayed that scene over and over with friends, acquaintances and eventually strangers. One by one they came to my house, and one by one they died there.

After several months, Henry had his lawyers draw up the paperwork to name me the sole owner of the house.

Peter West is the reason that house became my property. It would not be the blessed place that it is if it had not first hosted Peter's torture and his death. Henry cannot see it that way and that is Henry's to sort out. I think that even after thirty-six years, Henry and I are still sorting it out. If it is ever to be sorted.

Silence.

Eric I can't imagine what those years were like. I don't even know how to . . .

I can *understand* what it was. But I cannot possibly *feel* what it was.

Walter Tell me the name of one of your closest friends.

Eric Tristan.

Walter Imagine that Tristan is dead. Name another.

Eric Jasper.

Walter Jasper is also dead.

Eric Jason.

Walter Jason has been at St Vincent's for two weeks. The toxoplasmosis has left him with dementia.

Eric Jason, his husband.

Walter Because they cannot legally be married, abandonment is simpler. Jason has left him.

Young Men Patrick is dead.

Alex is dead.

Colin is dead.

Lucas is infected.

Zach is dying from pneumocystis carinii.

Chris is healthy. His partner has just been diagnosed.

You just visited Mark in the hospital. Tonight you will visit Will.

Tomorrow is Eddie's funeral.

Michael's body is covered with KS lesions.

Jeffrey is infected but asymptomatic.

Nick is dead.

Daniel is dead.

Stephen is infected.

Brian's partner has peripheral neuropathy. He screams in pain at the slightest touch.

Scott is in Paris, hoping to get HPA-23.

Javier went home to die in his mother's house.

Jonathan's family won't take him back.

Brandon is dead.

Matthew is dead.

Leo is infected.

Kurt is infected but he doesn't know it. David, his partner, will find out first.

Frankie's sister calls you to tell you he's died.

Adam has disappeared altogether.

Phillip is dead.

Trevor is dead.

Kevin is infected.

Rumors fly about incarcerations of gay men as a precaution.

Politicians begin to openly discuss mass quarantines.

There is talk of outlawing homosexuality, rumors of deportations.

Anti-gay violence is on the rise.

The American public becomes galvanized by the epidemic: not against the illness but against the people who have it.

Businesses cancel health insurance policies for employees with AIDS.

States pass legislation requiring home sellers to divulge if a person with AIDS has ever lived there.

Sam is dead.

Mark is dead.

Miguel is infected.

Paul has it.

Ben has it.

Carlos has it.

Wesley is dead.

Caleb is dead.

David is dead.

James is dead.

Andrew is dead.

Jacob is dead.

Walter That is what it was.

End of Act One.

Act Two

Autumn 2016

SCENE ONE

1. Chicago Club / Eric and Toby's Apartment

Thumping house music. A group of men dancing. Toby is in the middle of them. So is Adam. Toby's phone vibrates in his pocket. He looks at it, makes his way off the floor.

Toby Fair warning: I'm drunk and stoned and I also might be rolling.

Eric Oh my God, Toby. One drug at a time!

Toby Tom gave us each a Molly. The man is a fucking CVS. Hi!

Eric Yes you are. I'm two minutes away from turning thirty-four.

Toby It's only eleven.

Eric Time zones, baby. You're an hour behind in Chicago.

Toby Oh, right! I set a reminder for midnight. I wouldda called too late. Or too early?

Eric Where are you?

Toby A bunch of us decided to go out dancing. It's like I'm eighteen years old again and sneaking into Limelight.

Eric Is Adam with you?

Toby He is!

Eric Give him a big hug for me.

Toby Will do!

Eric Are you taking care of him?

Toby He's not a child, Eric.

Eric He's younger than he thinks.

Toby What are you doing tomorrow? Anything fun?

Eric The Lads are coming over for brunch. I'm introducing them to Walter.

Toby You and Walter seem to be spending a lot of time together. Should I be jealous?

Eric Yes, very. He's had quite a life. I've been getting a little first-hand gay history from him.

Toby Listen, it's chilly out and I'm scantily clad. I'll call you tomorrow, okay?

Eric Okay. I love you, Toby.

Toby Yeah, me too, babe. Byeeee! Happy birthday!

He hangs up and returns to the club, diving back into the middle of the crowd.

2. *Adam's Apartment in Chicago*

Adam Fuck, I'm still rolling.

Toby You can't still be rolling.

Adam Your eyes are so beautiful.

Toby Okay, you're still rolling.

Adam I love you, Toby.

Toby That's my cue to go.

Adam No, let's stay up and talk.

Toby It's four-thirty in the morning.

Adam goes into the bathroom.

You're not about to throw up, are you?

Adam I think I have to pee.

The shower starts offstage.

Toby Are you taking a shower?

Adam (*off*) What?

Toby Are you taking a shower?

Adam (*off*) I'm going to take a quick shower.

Toby I think it's sweet that you brought a framed photo of you and your parents.

Adam (*off*) What?

Toby Can you even hear me right now?

Adam (*off*) What?

Toby Then I'll only say this once: I think you're really amazing.

Adam (*off*) I can't hear a word you're saying, Toby.

Toby Good.
     Watching you rehearse these last few weeks, to see Elan come to life in that room, to watch you become him . . . you're so very good in this play, Adam . . . and in the few more moments that I can say these things, I just want you to know that you amaze me, Adam. And I really wanna fuck you right now.

The shower stops. Adam enters with a towel wrapped around his waist.

Adam I wanna ask you something.

Toby Okay . . .

Adam How am I doing? In the part, I mean. As Elan.

Toby It's early days.

Adam I can't get a firm grip on him at times, you know what I mean?

Toby You're still figuring him out.

Adam I mean, he's kind of a dick, you know? And I love that about him. But he can be a little cocky and manipulative.

Toby Right.

Adam So . . . I dunno. I just don't want the audience not to like me.

Toby Trust me, Adam. The audience is going to like you. I wouldn't overthink it. Just remember he ain't no virgin.

Adam You don't think *I'm* a virgin, do you?

Toby God, I hope you're not.

Adam Far from it.

Toby Oh 'far', huh? How far, exactly?

Adam You mean in years or in . . . ?

Toby Cocks. How far from virginity are you in erect penises? If you lined them up end to end, how far to the moon could you get?

Adam Probably not as far as you. I guess you've had a lot of sex in your life, huh?

Toby I'm Cape fuckin' Canaveral, baby.

Adam You're probably more like Elan in that regard than I am.

Adam removes the towel, standing there naked.

Toby Here's what I'll say: if Elan stepped out of the shower and stood before me completely naked, he wouldn't then pussyfoot around about what he wanted, he'd just come right out and say it. That, I think, is the main difference between you and the character that I've written. I should get to bed.

A moment, then Adam puts on underwear.

We need to take you shopping for better underwear.

Adam What's wrong with my underwear?

Toby It looks like you bought it at Costco.

Adam But . . . I did.

Toby Gay men shouldn't shop at Costco until they're at least forty and own land. What if you'd hooked up tonight? You really want a guy seeing you in that Fruit-of-the-Loom banality you're wearing right now?

Adam Why do you always pick on me?

Toby (*mocking mimicking*) 'Why do you always pick on me?'
I tease you, there's a difference.

Adam Why can't you just be nice to me?

Toby I *am* nice to you.

Adam You're always making fun of how rich and spoiled I am. Sometimes I think you don't like me.

Toby Oh come on, Adam. Don't be such a baby.

Adam I'm not a baby. Stop calling me that.

Toby You have to know that you've lived a pretty protected life.

Adam Is that my fault?

Toby No, not at all. But I hope you realize it's, like, a one-in-a-million life you're living.

Adam I know I'm very fortunate.

Toby I'm hard on you because someone needs to be. You can't expect the world to coddle you the way mommy does. You can't expect to get what you want just because you want it. You can't coast through life without some kind of adversity.

Adam You know I was adopted, right?

Toby Oh shut up, you were not.

    A beat.

Were you?

Adam I was born in Arkansas. My mother was sixteen. She left me at the hospital. My parents adopted me when I was two weeks old.

Toby Adam, I'm sorry. It's a one-in-a-*billion* life you're living.

    Adam shoves Toby.

Adam Fuck you, Toby.

Toby That's the spirit.

    Adam shoves Toby again.

Adam Why can't you encourage me?

Toby Because you get enough of that in your life.

Adam But I want it from you.

Toby It bothers me when privileged people pretend that they know what it's like to struggle or be scared to death.

    He releases Adam.

Toby Goodnight, Adam.

He moves to the door.

Adam I once got fucked in a bathhouse in Prague.

Toby You did not.

Adam Okay then, I didn't.

Morgan Did you?

Toby Oh, I see: is this your way of proving to me that you're not a virgin? I didn't really think that you were.

Adam I went to Prague over Christmas break my senior year. My boyfriend and I had just broken up, I felt a little lost and heartbroken and so I booked a flight and went.

Toby And what, pray tell, did you do while mending your broken widdle heart in Prague?

Adam I went to museums. I drank in cafés and smoked way too many cigarettes. Then one night I worked up the courage to go to a bathhouse, just to see what it was like.

Toby What *was* it like?

Adam It was hot.

Toby Oh come on. If you're going to tell a writer about a visit to a Czech bathhouse, you should at least do him the courtesy of using better adjectives.

Adam My heart pounds in my chest as I ride the metro there from my hotel. My hands tremble with fear as I present / my ID at the door.

Toby Get to the good stuff. If there isn't a dick in your mouth in the next minute, I'm leaving.

Adam I found a hot tub that's empty and I get in.

Toby Okay, so you're in the tub . . .

Adam And this one guy comes over and gets into the tub with me. He reaches down and grabs my dick. I let him stroke me off for a while but I'm not really into it so I get up and leave.

Toby The bathhouse?

Adam No, just the room. I go downstairs into this dark, warm, tiled room. It's basically a long hallway with stalls on either side. The first thing I notice is the sound of moaning. I start to walk down the corridor, passing each stall. Some are empty. Some have one or a couple of guys jerking off or sucking each other off. I remove my towel and walk down the corridor, looking into each of the stalls as I go.

Toby Were you hard?

Adam The hardest.

Toby Did anybody notice you?

Adam Some look up as I pass.

Toby Where did you go then?

Adam I get to this one stall and I find these two guys fucking. I stand there and watch. I'd never seen two people having sex before, outside of porn. They both smile and invite me over.

Toby And what happened?

Adam The guy getting fucked starts sucking me off.

Toby Wow. Really?

Adam Then the guy who was fucking him pulls out and joins him.

Toby They're both sucking you off?

Adam Yeah, back and forth. Both mouths on me at once.

Their hands are all over me. I look up and see three other guys in the entryway, watching.

Toby What did you do?

Adam I invite them over.

Toby You did not.

Adam They start feeling my body. They take turns sucking me off. More guys start to show up.

Toby How many?

Adam Eventually? Maybe fifteen, twenty?

Toby You're making this up.

Adam Am I?

Toby Are you?
Go on.

Adam They're all sucking me off, rubbing my body, eating me out, kissing me all over. They're all exploring me, feeling me. Worshipping me.

Toby How did that feel?

Adam I felt like the most desirable person in the world. I felt like a god.
Then there's this one guy. So hot, all muscle. He whispers something into my ear. I just smile and nod. Then before I knew what was happening, he slides inside me and starts to fuck me.

Toby Stop it.
Go on.

Adam Everyone just stands by and watches while this really hot guy fucks me. So I decide to put on a show for them.

Toby How?

Adam I moan, I arch my back.

Toby God, I can only imagine what that looked like.

Adam Can you?

Toby I'm picturing it right now.

Adam How's it look?

Toby Really fucking good.

Adam Eventually another guy wants to take a turn.

Toby Did you let him?

Adam Yeah. So now this other guy and I are fucking. Then another guy takes a turn, then another. Eventually I lose count.

Toby Jesus, Adam.

Adam Meanwhile, everyone is touching me. Thirty hands, fifteen mouths on my body. It wasn't even me in that moment, it was this other version of me. I remember thinking to myself: 'This is what it feels to truly be alive.'

I start to get close. I stand up on a bench. By now I'm completely covered in sweat and lube and spit. I start to jack myself off, bringing myself closer and closer to orgasm. All eyes are on me. Wanting me, encouraging me, demanding of me that I cum for them. And then finally, standing over them, my world contracts into a tight little ball and I release myself . . . I spray my cum all over them, like I'm anointing them. I've never cum so hard or so much in all my life. It was the closest I've ever been to genuine ecstasy.

Toby reaches for Adam. Adam lets him.

Everyone starts to cum. It was beautiful to watch. I was euphoric. I felt like a cult leader. And I remember thinking: I always want to feel like I do right now. This moment, this feeling, I want to live in this moment for the rest of my life.

Toby continues to feel Adam.

Slowly my euphoria started to fade and a thought starts to form, like Adam Lucas McDowell returning to this hot, sweaty body: none of those guys had been wearing condoms. And suddenly, I'm awoken from my dream to face the fact that I'd just barebacked with at least a dozen guys.

I got down off the bench and made my way out of the stall. Everyone was grabbing at me, wanting me to stay. Suddenly their touches felt like violations.

Toby removes his hands from Adam's body.

I ran to the locker room and quickly dressed. I left with my clothes sticking to my body, still sweaty and covered in lube and spit and cum. I smelled so disgustingly. I ran to my hotel. When I got to my room, I took the hottest shower I could stand. I cleaned myself and discovered I was bleeding. I could see it going down the drain. I got out of the shower and looked at my clothes. There was blood all over my underwear and inside my jeans.

Toby What did you do?

Adam I called my mom.

Toby You told your mother / what you did?!

Adam I just told her it was one guy. She called a friend of hers, a surgeon at Sloan-Kettering. This surgeon called a friend of his in Prague, who wrote me a prescription for PEP. I flew home the next day and we went up to Vermont for Christmas. I got really sick on Christmas Day. It felt like the worst flu ever. My mother took me to the hospital where I got a rapid HIV test. It came back inconclusive. The doctor ordered bloodwork. But it was Christmas and

I had to wait three days for the lab to re-open. Worst Christmas of my life. Three days later, my mom and I drove back to the hospital for the results. They found the virus in my blood. Trace amounts. Barely detectable. But still detectable. HIV positive.

Toby I had no idea.

Adam The doctor told me to keep taking the PEP treatment for the rest of the month. I went back to school and tried to distract myself with work. I would lay awake at night obsessively going over that night in my mind. Which one gave this to me? How could an experience that transcendent yield consequences so terrifying? Once the month was out, I went to the health center on campus. They did another round of tests. This time they came back negative across the board.

Toby Oh. So . . . what does that mean, exactly?

Adam It means I was exposed to the virus, I became temporarily HIV positive and the PEP treatment worked. It means I came as close to the edge as possible and at the last second I was rescued. Kinda like what my parents did for me when I was two weeks old.

Silence.

Don't ever tell me that I don't know what it's like to be scared to death.

Toby Adam, I –

Adam It's getting late.

Toby Adam, I –

Adam I should get to bed.

Toby Adam –

Adam Night, Toby.

Toby silently stands, grabs his jacket and makes his way to the door.

Toby I'll, um, I'll see you tomorrow.

Morgan That night, Adam McDowell learned an important lesson. He had power. Far more than he ever imagined.

Young Man 1 He wondered what else he might be capable of.

End of Scene One.

SCENE TWO

October 9, 2016. Eric's Thirty-Fourth Birthday

Morgan Eric awoke on his thirty-fourth birthday to an email from the Glass family's attorney. In exchange for a settlement, the Glass family had agreed to vacate the property at midnight on December 31. Eric busied himself with preparations for his birthday brunch, pushing thoughts of the future to the back of his mind.

Eric His friends arrived at eleven.

1. Eric and Toby's Apartment

Eric, Walter, Tristan, Jasper, Jason 1 and Jason 2 at Eric's dining table. Jason 1 and Jason 2 are showing Walter pictures of their wedding.

Jason 2 And that's us in the garden before the ceremony.

Walter Lovely.

Jason 2 And that's us still in the garden before the ceremony.

Walter Very nice.

Jason 2 And that's us in the garden before the ceremony but from a different angle.

Walter Yes, I see that.

Jason 1 Let's show him the floral arrangements.

Jason 2 We had all our guests bring flowers in lieu of gifts.

Jason 1 I really wanted a Vitamix.

Jason 2 Or make donations to their favorite causes.

Jason 1 My uncle gave $250 to the NRA so that kinda backfired a bit. (*To Jason 2.*) I told you we should have sent a pre-approved list of charities.

Jason 2 Yes, but that would have been counter to the idea of an ethical, conscience-based, DIY wedding. The ceremony was performed by the guests themselves, Quaker-style.

Jason 1 Took almost two hours. Show him a picture of the dinner.

Jason 2 My friend Sarah is a vegan chef. Everything was raw, locally sourced, humanely harvested. She prepared the meal with the help of our students.

Jason 1 They each got their own knives, which we thought was a good idea at the time.

Jason 2 Oh, you only needed seven stitches.

Jasper Your partner is Henry Wilcox, right? The real estate developer.

Walter Yes, that's right.

Jason 1 How long have you been together?

Walter Over thirty-six years.

Jason 2 Wow!

Jason 1 Have you ever thought of getting married?

Walter No.

Jason 2 Why not?

Walter Never saw the need.

Jason 2 Yeah, but the party. And the gift registry.

Jason 1 But what happens if he dies before you? Do you ever worry about that?

Walter No.

Jason 2 Oh, this is one of my favorites. Look.

Walter Ah, still in the garden, are we?

Jason 2 It's such a lovely garden.

Tristan What do you do for a living, Walter?

Walter Fortunately, I've never needed to work. I raised Henry's sons for him, which was work enough.

Jason 1 You and your partner have children?

Walter Henry has two boys from his marriage. Their mother died when they were young.

Eric Really, Walter? I didn't know that.

Jason 2 Ooh, did you adopt them?

Walter No, but I raised them.

Jason 2 Well, speaking of adopting . . . (*To Jason 1.*) Should we tell them?

Jason 1 I think you just did, babe.

Jason 2 Jason and I are adopting a baby in the new year.

The Lads react excitedly.

Jason 1 It's still not completely certain.

Jason 2 But we found a mother. She lives in Phoenix. She's due early January.

Eric God, you guys are gonna be parents.

Jason 1 If everything works out.

Walter Do all of you plan to have children?

Jason 1 ⎤ Obviously we do.

Jason 2 ⎥ We're gonna have three!

Tristan ⎥ I'd like to some day.

Jasper ⎦ No fucking way.

Walter Why not for you, Jasper?

Jasper Children are dirty, diseased bloodsuckers who get their grubby little fingers all over your expensive furniture. They drain you of your vitality, rob you of your sleep, age you prematurely, and then resent you for it on their therapist's couch, which you have to pay for.

Walter Well, as long as you've given it some thought.

Jasper If I ever do find the person I'm meant to be with, I wanna fuck him senseless every day. Go mountain climbing. Have an orgy in the Pines. Fist a twink together.

Jason 2 Well *you're* not babysitting.

Jasper Yes I am!

Eric Let's eat!

Young Man 4 The brunch commenced and Walter withdrew into silence.

Walter lights a cigarette. Stunned silence from Eric and the Lads. Walter notices.

Walter Do you mind if I smoke?

They all clearly do, but:

Eric I don't mind. (*To the rest.*) Do you?

Tristan I don't mind.

Jasper No.

Jason 2 I'm expecting a child. (*Then:*) I don't mind.

Young Man 3 Eric was afraid Walter wasn't enjoying himself nearly as much as he was enjoying his cigarette.

Young Man 1 And so he attempted to bring the subject around to a topic about which he was certain Walter would have some insight.

Eric You know what I miss? I miss the feeling that being gay was like being a member of a secret club.

Jason 2 You mean being in the closet?

Eric No, I mean that liminal state when we were out but also, I don't know, still kinda mysterious and opaque to society.

Tristan Oh, like: friends were welcome to visit our little club but only members were allowed to access the full benefits.

Eric Yes! And in order to fully join, you needed people to help bring you in.

Jason 2 You've just described SoHo House.

Tristan No.

Eric No, I'm describing a community. Everything was a little secretive, you know?

Tristan But not in a shameful way –

Eric No.

Tristan   – more like in a 'this is our thing' kinda way.

Eric Yes! It was a secret culture with a secret language and shared, secret experiences.

Tristan That really was the best part of being gay, wasn't it?

Jasper I always thought the best part was the orgasms.

Jason 2 Being gay doesn't feel remarkable anymore. It's like, 'Oh you're gay? Ho-hum, what other tricks can you do?'

Jasper But the point of all that work at visibility was to not feel stigmatized. To not have our sexual identities be our primary identities.

Jason 2 I never felt stigmatized, I felt *special*! I *like* being gay.

Jason 1 But being gay isn't all you are, baby. You're a teacher, you're married, you're about to become one goddamn sexy father.

Eric I think my question is: what does it mean now to be a gay man?

Tristan There was never one answer to that question.

Eric No, of course not. But there were several clearly identifiable cultural markers.

Jason 2 Are you talking about drag queens and camp and being Friends of Dorothy?

Eric Yes, in part.

Jason 2 About seeing every revival of *Gypsy* since at least Tyne Daly?

Jasper But that's just a clichéd part of the gay identity.

Eric I just mean there are certain identifiable, broadly applicable cultural markers that are specific to the gay community that I fear we are starting to lose.

Tristan For example?

Eric Um . . . well, take camp, for instance.

Jasper Ugh, I hate camp. It's like gay minstrelsy. I'm so happy we're past that.

Jason 2 I'm not past it. I like camp.

Jasper Of course you do.

Jason 2 Yeah, because I'm a big fucking nelly faggot queen and I do not care who knows it.

Jasper Yasss kween!

Tristan Oh! *That* is something that genuinely pisses me off: this whole 'yas queen' thing. My fourteen-year-old niece said 'Yass kween' at Thanksgiving last year and I was like, 'Who the fuck have you been hanging out with?' and she was all like –

Young Man 4 'Oh Uncle Tristan, that's from *Broad City*.'

Tristan And I was like, 'The hell it is. That phrase has been toppling out of the painted lips of drag queens since before you were born.' They have taken a phrase that started in the drag world and built a brand off it.

Eric Our culture is being co-opted.

Jasper But you can't on the one hand demand visibility and then cry foul when your culture starts getting disseminated into the culture at large.

Eric That's only true if that kind of cultural visibility also comes with the kind of societal participation that matters.

Jasper Such as . . .?

Eric Such as . . .

Tristan Come on, baby, you got this.

Eric Okay. Harvey Milk!

Lads react loudly.

Tristan Oh God, Eric just played the Harvey Milk card!

Eric I mean, sure it's great Sean Penn won an Oscar for playing Harvey Milk but American students are still taught nothing about queer history. It feels like we're getting stripped for parts and the inside is hollowing out. It feels like the community that I came up in is slowly fading away. When was the last time any of us actually hung out at a gay bar?

Jason 2 They're all closing.

Eric My point exactly! Gay bars used to be safe spaces for people like us to be ourselves and to find others like us. Now everyone just goes onto Grindr. But what about a twenty-year-old kid who's not looking for sex, but rather for community, for a connection with something that helps him understand himself? Or the sixty-year-old man who's looking for the same?

Jasper Or the sixty-year-old who's looking for the twenty-year-old?

Tristan That's gonna be you.

Eric What happens to that shared culture? If being gay only describes who we love and who we fuck but not also how we encounter the world, then gay culture and gay community would start to disappear. And we still need that community. Because this country is still filled with people who hate us with vengeful, murderous fanaticism.

88

Jason 1 'Vengeful, murderous fanaticism'? I think you may be going a little overboard. Look at where we are now. Progress has *happened*.

Tristan Tell that to the kids at Pulse.

Jason 1 I know. I don't mean to minimize that.

Tristan But . . .

Jason 1 No, my point is that there will always be vengeful, murderous fanatics in the world. Be they homophobes, racists, transphobes, you name it. That will never change. What can change, what has changed and what must continue to change is the way our society *protects* people from vengeful, murderous fanatics. I mean, I think it's fair to stipulate that, barring an unforeseen tragedy, we in this room are generally less vulnerable than others in our community.

Tristan I don't know if it is fair to say that.

Jason 1 Are you saying that you, Tristan, a well-educated medical professional aren't at least marginally less vulnerable than, say, a homeless queer teenager?

Tristan Okay, yes – I do stipulate that.

Jason 1 Right. Just as Rachel Maddow might stipulate that she is in some ways less vulnerable than you.

Jason 2 Would she, though? She's a gay woman.

Jason 1 She's a *rich* gay woman with a national media platform.

Jason 2 Fair.

Jason 1 Okay! So – who do we have? We have Rachel Maddow, Tristan, a homeless queer teenager. Oh! And I guess if we wanted to be completely accurate about it, we could say Mitt Romney, Rachel Maddow, Tristan, a homeless queer teenager.

Tristan Where would you put Laverne Cox?

Jason 1 In the White House.

Jason 2 Where would you put Matt Bomer?

Jason 1 On my face.

Jasper What about Peter Thiel?

Jason 1 Fuck Peter Thiel.
I guess you'd probably say Mitt Romney, fuck Peter Thiel, Matt Bomer on my face, Rachel Maddow, Laverne Cox –

Eric Laverne Cox before Tristan?

Jason 1 She has a fucking Emmy. Okay, so we have Mitt Romney, fuck Peter Thiel, Matt Bomer, Rachel Maddow, Laverne Cox in the White House, Tristan, a homeless queer teenager . . .

Walter (*singing*) And a partridge in a pear tree. (*Then:*) Sorry. Please continue.

Jason 1 I forgot where I was. Where was I?

Jason 2 Matt Bomer on my face?

Eric Vengeful, murderous fanatics.

Jason 1 Yes! Thank you! Now we have a chance to build on the progress that has been made in the last eight years. How do the people in this room – who have largely benefited from the Obama years – continue to fight for the community that has always fought for us? What happens now?

Jasper Now let's talk about trans rights.

Jason 2 Let's finally ratify the motherfuckin' ERA.

Tristan Let's talk about the resurgence of HIV among gay men of color.

Eric Let's talk about the rising rates of addiction, suicide and homelessness among LGBT youth.

Jason 1 Yes! These are the things that will require just as much of our blood, sweat and tears as marriage equality did. And these are the things we have the chance to make some real progress on once Clinton is elected.

Walter Are we that certain she's going to win?

The Lads seem sure.

What happens if you're wrong?

Jason 2 ⎞ Read the polls!

Jason 1 ⎪ Nate Silver is never wrong.

Jasper ⎬ It's the Senate we should be focused on, anyway.

Tristan ⎠ There's no way she's not gonna win.

Eric I think what Walter means to say is that we should never assume anything, right, Walter?

Walter In part. I'm also afraid she's going to lose.

Silence.

I'm sorry. It's Eric's birthday. And we're all having such a / nice time.

Eric No, it's probably worth thinking about: what if the unthinkable happens?

Tristan ⎞ My girl's gonna win!

Jason 2 ⎪ It's gonna be a blowout.

Jasper ⎬ We're gonna take Arizona this year.

Jason 1 ⎠ I set my watch by Nate Silver's predictions.

Eric But what if it does? We need our community, we need our history. How else can we teach the next generation who they are and how they got here? Human culture from time immemorial has been transmitted through stories, right? Think about the ancient epics: the *Odyssey*, the *Mahabharata*, oral histories that allowed cultures to understand themselves. In order to become an honorable Greek, one had to study the actions of Odysseus. A young Hindu would reflect on the conversation between Arjuna and Krishna on the battlefield. African-Americans teach their children about slavery and Jim Crow and the Civil Rights Movement so that they will understand Freddie Grey, Sandra Bland, and Trayvon Martin. Just as my family taught me about the Holocaust. And from this intergenerational conversation, passed along in some cases for millennia, history is conveyed and cultures survived. Greeks thump their chests and reflect on the invasion of Troy. Black children stand just a little taller at the mention of Rosa Parks. And we in our own culture feel the stirring of pride when we reflect on the meaning of Stonewall, Edie Windsor, Bayard Rustin, Harvey Milk and the bravery of the men and women on the front lines of the epidemic. And to let that go means we've relinquished a part of ourselves. If we can't have a conversation with our past, then what will be our future? Who are we? And more importantly: who will we become?

Morgan And then, Eric thought but did not say:

Eric Who will *I* become?

2. *Hallway*

Walter I had such a wonderful time.

Eric No you didn't, you hated it.

Walter I did not. You all lead such interesting lives.

Eric We lead the lives of gibbering monkeys.

Walter No, you're all so exciting to listen to. It's been years since I've been in a room with younger gay men. You all give me such hope. And I found what you in particular had to say was incredibly thoughtful and moving.

Eric Just the after-effects of three glasses of wine.

Walter It felt more like a *cri de coeur*.

Eric Just grandstanding to show off my education.

Walter Don't, Eric. Do not discount my words the way you discount yourself.

Eric I wasn't trying / to dis—

Walter You have so much promise, Eric Glass. I admire you tremendously. I see in you a version of myself I had long since forgotten.

Eric Walter – I don't know what to say to that.

Walter When I don't know what to say I find it's best to say nothing.

Eric That honestly has never occurred to me. I can't tell you what your friendship has meant to me this autumn.

Walter does not answer – lost, it seems, in reverie.

Walter?

Walter I would very much like to show you my house upstate.

Eric Yes, I would love that. We should take a trip sometime.

Walter How about tonight?

Eric Tonight?

Walter Yes. Right now. The cherry tree should be in full reds and oranges. It'll do us both good.

Eric I would love to see it.

Walter Wonderful.

Eric It's just that tonight's not . . . tonight's not the –
Yes. I would love to see your house tonight.

Walter There's a train at 7:30. If we hurry we can make it.

*The ding of an elevator. Two strapping, all-American
young men enter: Charles and Paul Wilcox, Henry's
sons. They argue between themselves.*

Charles You're gonna get a ticket, Paul.

Paul You're crazy. The hydrant was ten feet away.

Charles Hey, there he is!

Walter Charlie? Paul? What are you doing here?

Charles We're taking you to dinner.

Paul Charles wanted to surprise you.

Walter Eric, these are Henry's sons, Charles and Paul.

Eric It's so nice to meet you. / I've heard so much about
you.

Charles What are you doing in the hallway?

Paul Are you locked out?

Walter No, we were just leaving to go up to my house.

Paul I'll call a locksmith.

Paul takes out his phone, dials.

Charles What, upstate? No, it's way too late. We're taking
you to dinner.

Paul (*into his phone*) Susie, get me a locksmith. Walter's
locked out of the apartment again.

Walter No, Paul, I'm not locked out –

Charles I booked your favorite table at La Grenouille.

Paul (*to Susie*) There might be a spare in Pop's office.

Walter I promised Eric I'd show him the house.

Charles You're not going to say no to us, are you? We haven't seen you in weeks.

Walter (*to Eric*) I'm so sorry – I didn't know they were coming.

Eric It's fine. We can go another time.

Paul (*into the phone*) What do you mean 'What do they look like?' They're keys. They look like keys.

Walter Eric, you should come with us. It's his birthday today.

Eric Oh, no. I don't want to intrude.

Walter It won't be any intrusion.

Charles He doesn't want to intrude. Come on, Walter. Paul parked in front of a hydrant.

Paul (*to Charles*) That hydrant was twenty feet away. (*To Susie.*) Call me back if you find them. (*To Charles.*) She can't find the keys. (*To Eric.*) Who the fuck are you?

Walter Eric, are you sure you don't want to join us?

Eric It wasn't meant to for us to go tonight.

Walter I'm so sorry. Thank you for understanding.

Charles Walter, let's go.

Paul Who the fuck is that guy?

Walter I won't forget my promise to you.

Walter, Charles and Paul exit.

End of Scene Two.

Autumn 2016

Young Man 1 But it seemed that Walter *had* forgotten his promise. In the weeks following Eric's birthday, Eric saw little of Walter. He was rarely home whenever Eric visited and, whenever Eric did catch him in, Walter was never in the mood for more than a cursory exchange of pleasantries.

Toby Eric flew to Chicago to attend the opening of Toby's play.

1. 'Loved Boy' Opens

Morgan The play received ecstatic reviews.

Young Man 7 The director Tom Durrell's staging was deemed revelatory.

Young Man 1 Adam's performance was hailed as one of the most thrilling stage debuts that anyone could remember.

Young Man 8 It was said in those weeks that the most dangerous place to be was in between Adam and any agent hoping to sign him.

Young Man 1 The production was a hit.

Young Man 2 Offers were made and plans were hatched for a Broadway transfer the following autumn.

Toby Toby was hailed as the premier writer of his generation. His talents were breathlessly compared to Salinger, Albee, Eugene O'fucking-Neill.

Morgan No.

Toby Why not?

Morgan Because then what?

Toby Then? He lives happily ever after!

Morgan No, the response to Toby's writing was decidedly less effusive than that.

Toby How much less?

Young Man 1 His talent was recognized but the achievement was not considered as great as his colleagues'.

Morgan The impression one got was that Toby Darling had crafted the perfect vehicle for Tom Durrell and Adam McDowell to prove their genius.

Toby That's bullshit.

Morgan And yet, that is what happened.

Toby They didn't say one positive thing about the writing? Nothing to indicate that Toby deserved any credit for this success? After all that work? After all these years?

Young Man 1 Not in the way that Toby needed to hear.

Toby Well, fuck that. Toby flies to Los Angeles where, over the course of three dizzying weeks, he drops his longtime agent for a new team at a high-powered agency, he takes on a manager, lawyers up, and promptly sells the film rights to *Loved Boy*. (*To Morgan.*) *That's* what Toby does.

Young Man 8 Wouldn't Toby have made a lot more money if he waited until *after* it opened on Broadway to sell the film rights?

All eyes on Toby. Then:

Toby Fuck!

2. *November 8, 2016*

Eric On election night, Eric gathered with his friends to watch the returns –

Young Man 5 – while Toby had dinner with his new agents at Mr Chow's in Beverly Hills.

Young Man 6 Eric bought noisemakers and small American flags for the occasion.

Young Man 7 But from as early as seven o'clock, it was clear to Jasper that something was off.

Jasper Eric, I'm worried about Florida.

Eric Really?

Jasper Pinellas County is practically a dead heat right now. That shouldn't be happening.

Eric It's early yet, Jasper.

Jasper A Democrat should be leading by double digits in St Pete right out of the gate. And fuck, she's behind in Hillsboro County.

Morgan Eric texted Toby:

Eric Are you watching? Call me.

Jasper I'm telling you guys, this is not looking good.

Jason 1 Yeah, but Nate Silver still has her at 86 percent.

Jason 2 She just won Connecticut!

Eric Oh, and Massachusetts!

Morgan Nine o'clock:

Tristan Clinton takes New York!

Jasper Arizona, Colorado, Michigan, Minnesota, New Mexico, Wisconsin: all too close to call.

Morgan Ten o'clock:

Jasper Nevada too close to call. Utah too close to call.

Morgan And then at 10:21 . . .

Jasper Oh fuck, they just called Ohio.

Jason 1 Nate Silver has her at 72 percent.

Morgan 11:07 . . .

Jasper They just called North Carolina.

Jason 1 Sixty-seven percent.

Morgan And 11:30 . . .

Jasper Fuck, there goes Florida.

Jason 1 Fifty-three percent. Fuck you, Nate Silver!

Morgan Eric texted Toby:

Eric Where are you? This is bad. Is this really happening?

Morgan For hours, they watched with growing dread as state after state was called.

Jasper We still have a firewall in the Rust Belt. And Arizona might still be in play.

Morgan And then, nothing. Three hours of waiting as precinct after precinct slowly started to report. The Jasons went home. Tristan fell asleep in the guest room. Eric and Jasper finished another bottle of wine as they waited, waited for a miracle. And then at 3:04 in the morning . . .

Jasper They just called Pennsylvania. That's it, then. It's over.

Eric It's over.

Morgan A week later, Toby returned from Los Angeles.

3. *Eric and Toby's Apartment*

Toby You've known for a year we were losing this apartment and you didn't tell me?

Eric I've known it was a possibility.

Toby Why didn't you say anything / to me?

Eric I didn't want to worry you.

Toby Don't treat me like a child, Eric.

Eric I'm not, Toby / I simply . . .

Toby The night we got engaged, I mentioned having the wedding here at the apartment and you said 'Mmhmm, yeah maybe'. Did you know then?

Eric Yes.

Toby How long had you known?

Eric Only a couple of hours.

Toby You proposed to me the day you found out we were being evicted?

Eric The day I found out it was a possibility.

Toby You see how that looks, right?

Eric No . . .

Toby It looks like entrapment.

Eric How did I entrap you?

Toby By luring me into a marriage under false pretenses.

Eric Are you saying that if you *had* known about the apartment, you might have made a different decision?

Toby I'm saying that I didn't have all the information I needed when you asked me to marry you.

Eric What other information did you need? Are you with me because of this apartment?

Toby No!

Eric So then why should it matter?

Toby Because you weren't honest with me.

Eric I'm being honest with you now. We're going to have to move at the end of the year. I'm sorry I didn't say anything. I truly didn't want to worry you needlessly. But, with your advances on the play, I figure we might have just enough money for a down payment on a small apartment. We'll be like Jane Fonda and Robert Redford in *Barefoot in the Park*. Oh Toby, everything's going to be fine. At least now that you're back, we can finally start planning for the future.

Toby I can't just start looking at apartments with you, Eric. I can't just sit down and make plans for the future.

Eric Why not?

Toby Because who the fuck knows what going to happen between now and then? And in the meantime, I've got a lot of work to do. My play is coming to Broadway, I've got rewrites to do, I'm going to Los Angeles next week to have some meetings.

Eric You were just in Los Angeles / for three weeks!

Toby People wanna meet with me. What can I do? This is part of my business.

Eric And what about the part that's your life?

Toby I just can't make a commitment like that right now.

Eric Please Toby, just tell me what the fuck is going on?

Toby I don't want to get married. Okay? I don't want to get married.

Eric Right now?
   At all?
   Or to me?
   Toby?
   Toby please answer me.

Toby I don't know.

Eric Yes you do.

Toby I don't want to marry you.

Eric Why not?

Toby I just . . . I just feel we're in different places right now.

Eric What does that even mean, Toby?

Toby I don't –

Eric Please Toby, just be honest with me. I have done nothing but love and support you. I have walked beside you for seven years. I've even carried you at times.

Toby Okay, that is bullshit. You haven't carried me.

Eric You couldn't even afford a studio in Staten Island / when we met.

Toby You're going to throw that in my face?

Eric Now that I don't have this apartment to offer you / now that success is in your grasp, you don't need me anymore.

Toby It has nothing to do with your apartment!

Eric Maybe you even think you can do better. At least be honest and tell me that, Toby.

Toby I just want something different.

Eric Did you fuck Adam in Chicago?

Toby No!

Eric Do you want to fuck Adam?

Toby Yes! Of course I want to fuck Adam, who doesn't?

Eric I don't.

Toby Then there is something seriously wrong with you, Eric. He's gorgeous.

Eric There's more to people than beauty.

Toby You would have to tell yourself that, wouldn't you?
I'm sorry. I didn't mean that.

Eric Actually, that's the first honest thing you've said this entire conversation. And since we're finally telling each other the truth, you should know that I hated your fucking play.

Toby Wow, Eric. I never thought you would stoop so low as to lash out like that. That play is the greatest thing I've ever done in my life. We're a huge fucking hit and we're moving to Broadway!

Eric Because of Tom's production and Adam's performance.

Toby Oh fuck you, Eric. I worked my ass off on that play. I have been rolling that boulder up the hill for the last decade of my life.

Eric And who stood by your side while you were rolling your fucking boulder up the hill? You had the luxury of struggling for seven years because of me / and what I gave you.

Toby That is bullshit, Eric.
What you 'gave' me?' You didn't give me anything. I built my life from the ground up. God, I am so sick of

your holier-than-thou, thoughtful, sweet and kind fucking bullshit. You act like you're above the fray, can't be touched, fucking Yale, fucking Fieldston, fucking save the world by strongly worded Facebook post, when secretly you're just as manipulative and as self-involved and as frightened as the rest of us. But you slap on this veneer of middle-class perfection and you think that protects you from having to be a real person. But real people are ugly, Eric. Real people are compromised. Real people disappoint each other. Because the world is ugly and compromised and disappointing. And I'm sorry I can't be perfect like you. I was never given that option. I have no choice but to be a real person.

Eric That is the last thing that you are, Toby. You've become so good at spinning people / you think you can spin me, too.

Toby I don't 'spin' anyone.

Eric But I know that your book was a fraud from start to finish / and your play was –

Toby *Fraud?!* Fuck you, Eric.

Eric And your play was even worse. Not without talent, but worse: without truth. Toby, you are so afraid of actually being known – of really looking at yourself – that you have spent the last decade of your life constructing this elaborate narrative that has nothing to do with the truth. What happened to you as a child was unconscionable / and it hurts me every single day to know that it did.

Toby Don't you fucking dare / use that against me.

Eric But that was not the great tragedy of your life, Toby. No, the great tragedy of your life was denying that it *was* your life, and insisting on another at the expense of the truth. I couldn't even look at you after I saw your play.

Because it was a betrayal of the frightened little boy you once were. And soon all of New York is going to see it and I will be the only one who'll remember who you really are. And that's why you want to get as far away from me as possible: because I would remind you every day of what a fraud you are and what wasted potential your life has become. And that's what you're too much of a coward to say.

Silence.

Toby Well, Eric. If there's anyone who knows anything about wasted potential, it is you. And if you feel this way about me – if this is who you think I really am – then why the fuck did you stay with me for seven years?

Eric Because I love you, you fucking piece of shit!

Henry Wilcox enters.

Henry Am I interrupting something?

Toby ⎫ Yes.

Eric ⎭ No.

Eric Henry. Is everything all right?

Henry I wanted to come by to let you know . . . Walter's . . . Walter's gone.

Eric Gone?

Henry He died this morning.
Charles took him to the hospital yesterday. I flew back just in time to . . .
I know how close you and he had become while I was away.

Eric Henry, I don't even know what to say. I'm so sorry. Do you want to / come in?

Henry No, I . . . No. Thank you. I thought you'd want to know.

Eric Henry, I –

Henry exits. Toby cautiously approaches Eric.

Toby Eric.

Eric No!

Toby Eric, I'm sorry.

Eric You've ruined everything, Toby. Everything you touch, you ruin.

End of Scene Three.

SCENE FOUR

Autumn 2016

1. Henry and Walter's Apartment

Morgan Walter had been cremated, per his lifelong understanding with Henry. The doctors told of a body eaten entirely away by cancer. Walter had told no one of his illness. Not even Henry. Henry had already buried his parents, one sibling, the mother of his sons and friends far too numerous to count. But true mourning had largely eluded him. With Walter's passing, he could avoid it no longer. After thirty-six years together, Walter was gone. Henry's sons gathered at his apartment every evening.

Henry You don't have to come by every night.

Paul We were just in the neighborhood.

Charles Were you taking a nap?

Henry Yeah.

Charles Were you able to sleep?

Henry A little.

Charles Should I make some coffee?

Paul Maybe a drink.

Henry I'm fine, thank you.

Paul Everyone's been asking about you at the office.

Henry Shit. Are things falling apart already?

Paul No, that's not what I –

Charles Everyone just misses you, Pop.

Henry I should probably go in tomorrow, show my face.

Charles There's no rush.

Henry No, I'm done stewing. Walter wouldn't approve.

Charles No, it's true. He wouldn't.

Paul No.

Charles No.

Paul No.

Charles Nope.

Charles and Paul look at one another.

Henry What?

Charles A package arrived for you today. From a woman in Queens.

Paul She says she was Walter's nurse at the hospital.

Charles Inside was an envelope, with your name on it, in Walter's handwriting.

Morgan A chill trickled down Henry's spine. This was the closest these men had ever come to a spiritual communion with the dead.

Charles hands over Walter's letter. Henry opens it. It is as if he has seen a ghost.

Charles Pop, are you okay?

Paul What does it say?

Walter 'To Henry –
I should like Eric Glass to have my house.'

Charles *and* **Paul** That's it?

Henry That's it.

Paul Who the fuck is Eric Glass?

Henry He was a friend of Walter's. He and his partner live a few floors up. Apparently the two of them had spent a lot of time together while I was away.

Paul What do you mean 'spent time'?

Henry I just mean that Eric had been kind to Walter.

Charles Kind enough for Walter to leave him his house?

Paul This is bullshit – lemme see that. (*Grabbing it from Charles.*) But – it's written in pencil. Pencil doesn't count, does it?

Charles There's no date, it isn't witnessed. There's not even a signature.

Henry It's Walter's handwriting.

Charles It's not a legal document, Pop.

Henry It's his last request.

Charles Why would he leave that house to a total stranger? He loved that house.

Paul Hey – I bet this Glass guy tricked Walter into writing that.

Charles Yes! He probably knew that Walter was sick.

Paul Yes! Have you checked Walter's bank account lately?

Charles Yes! He's probably cleared him out already.

Paul The fucker. (*Pulling out his phone.*) We should call the cops.

Charles Yes!

Henry All right, both of you, that's enough.

Charles Come on, Pop. Don't you think this is just a little suspicious?

Henry Walter was always giving away books and knick-knacks to people.

Paul But never a fuckin' house!

Charles He was on so much morphine at the end.

Paul That fucking nurse should be fired for it.

Henry If Eric had needed somewhere to live, I could understand it. And even if he did, he wouldn't want to live up there.

Paul It's three hours from the city. We don't even go there anymore.

Charles That's not the point, Paul. That house is a part of our family. And it meant everything to Walter. He couldn't have meant to give it to a stranger.

Paul So then what do we do?

Charles looks at his father for a tacit go-ahead and then pulls out a lighter and sets the letter aflame.

Morgan Refrain, if you can, from judging the Wilcoxes too harshly. Should they have offered their home to Eric?

Logic – and even emotion – suggests not. What they could not have known was that to Walter it had been more than a house: it had been a spiritual possession, for which he sought a spiritual heir. No; the Wilcox men are not to be blamed for their decision.

Except.

One hard fact remains. They did neglect a personal appeal. The man who had died did say to them, 'Do this,' and they answered, 'We will not.'

End of Act Two.

Act Three

Autumn 2016–Spring 2017

SCENE ONE

1. Adam's Apartment

Toby on Adam's doorstep, soaking wet.

Toby Is this a bad time?

Adam You're soaked.

Toby Oh. Yeah.

Adam Let me get you a towel.

Toby That's okay.

Adam You're dripping on the rug.

Toby Sorry for barging in on you like this.

Adam It's fine. What's going on?

Toby Eric and I broke up tonight.

Adam *Wait, what?!* How? / What happened?

Toby I could really use a drink right now.

Adam Um, sure. Do you want some wine / or –

Toby Wine's a nice girl but she's no match for tonight.
I need whiskey. Lots of it. And bring me something while
I wait for it.

Adam Oh Toby.

   Adam pours Toby a drink.

Toby 'Oh Toby.' I'm going to have that phrase *emblazoned* on my tombstone.

Adam hands Toby the drink.

Adam What happened?

Toby Eric and I had the Hiroshima of fights.

Adam What about?

Toby You.

Morgan But what Toby actually said was:

Toby The thing is I can't even remember. All I know is that I told him I didn't want to get married.

Adam Oh Toby.

Toby There it is again: 'Oh Toby.' This time with judgement attached.

Adam Not judgement . . . bewilderment. You're Eric and Toby.

Toby Toby and Eric.
    I just felt stifled, you know? Eric has this whole future mapped out for us. Marriage, children, a house in fucking Westchester ten minutes from his parents.

Adam That sounds amazing.

Toby Then *you* marry him.

Adam You two love each other.

Toby Sometimes that's just not enough.

Adam I can't believe that. Because if you and Eric can't make things work, what hope is there for me?

Toby Oh, don't put that on me. I can't be a role model for you.

Adam I'm sure it's fixable.

Toby He fucking kicked me out, can you believe it? Jesus, I'm homeless.

Adam Do you still love Eric?

Toby I don't know anything right now. I think I might be a monster.

Adam Go home. Talk to him.

Toby God no. I'm sure he's summoned the coven by now. They're probably gathered in the apartment doing incantations against me. I'll probably get a hotel.

Adam I mean, you can stay here if you want. My parents are in Vermont.

Toby Yeah, okay. I'm sorry to drop all this on you.

Adam It's what friends do, right?

Toby Like I fuckin' know.

Adam And in the morning you'll call him and you'll work this out.

Toby The thing is, Adam, I don't want to work it out.

Adam What do you want, then, Toby?

Toby You.

Morgan But what Toby actually said was:

Toby I don't know anymore. I'm sorry I haven't been in touch since you got back from Chicago. Things have been nuts lately.

Adam I've been a little nuts, too.

Toby Yeah? Doing what?

Adam Been meeting with agents and managers, mostly.

Toby Yeah, me too. I just got back from LA.

Adam I'm going there next week.

Toby The old couch and water tour. The Evian Trail. Hey, I sold the film rights.

Adam Oh good for you, Toby!

Toby Yeah. Good for good ol' Toby.

Adam Wait, you sold the film rights *before* Broadway? Wouldn't you have made more / money if you'd –

Toby Just shut up, Adam. Hit me again.

Adam I got the offer for Broadway yesterday.

Toby Hey, that's great! I'm glad that all worked out.

  A beat.

Adam What do you mean 'worked out'?

Toby That they ended up going with you, after all.

Adam Why wouldn't they?

Toby What? Oh. There was talk of replacing you but that idea went nowhere.

Adam Who wanted to replace me?

Toby No one, just the producers. Don't worry, you're fine. I insisted that they keep you. Glad to hear they made the offer.

Adam Which of the producers wanted to replace me?

Toby Oh God, I shouldn't have said anything. There was the briefest talk of finding a star but that fizzled very quickly.

Adam Tom told me everyone was excited for me to do the show in New York. That I was the star.

Toby You talked to Tom recently?

Adam We talk on the phone. Text, you know.

Toby I didn't realize you two were that close.

Adam Oh. Well . . .

Toby What?

Adam Well . . . I've been meaning to tell you, actually. Tom and I are . . . we're kinda dating.

Toby You and . . . Tom?

Adam Yeah.

Toby He's fifty years old.

Adam He's forty-seven. I wanted to tell you but . . . you've been so busy. It started just after we opened. I didn't think that he – anyway, it took us both by surprise.

Toby starts to implode.

Toby, are you okay? Toby?

Toby You're fucking Tom Durrell?

Adam Toby –

Toby You're fucking the director of my play?

Adam He's my director, too.

Toby Which is why you shouldn't be fucking him!

Adam I mean, it's more than just sex. We . . . we kinda fell in love.

Toby Oh I don't believe this. You're in love with Tom Durrell?

Adam I think I might be. He's taking me to Brazil for Christmas.

Toby I don't even know what to say to you right now.

Adam You could try being happy for me.

Toby Yeah, but Tom fucking Durrell, Adam?

Adam What's wrong with Tom?

Toby What's wrong with *me*?

Adam Toby?

Toby tries to kiss Adam. Adam pulls away.

Toby.

Toby grabs Adam and pulls him toward him. Adam resists.

Toby, stop.

Toby pulls Adam in once more. Again Adam resists.

Toby, get off of me!

Toby pulls him back once more into a kiss.

Toby, stop!

Adam shoves him off, knocking him off balance and to the floor.

Why did you do that?

Toby Because I love you.

Adam No you don't.

Toby I love you.

Adam Stop saying that.

Toby I ended things with Eric because of you.

Adam No, that isn't true.

Toby Yes it is! I came here tonight to tell you that.

Adam No you didn't. That's not why you came here.

Toby Please, you have to believe me. My heart was pure. My heart is always pure. Unfortunately it happens to be surrounded by the rest of me.

Adam You're upset and and and you're confused –

Toby I love you.

Adam And you're drunk.

Toby I've been in love with you since that night I walked you home in the rain.

Adam Toby, we're friends. Eric is like my brother.

Toby That's what's made all of this so agonizing. I fell in love with you and I kept falling in love with you and now I'm completely, irreparably, disastrously in love with you. You have to know that, Adam. I think that maybe you feel the same.

Adam No, I don't.

Toby Don't feel like you have to be in any rush to answer.

Adam I don't feel the same as you.

Toby Maybe you're confused.

Adam I am not confused. I do not love you, Toby. In fact, I want you to leave.

Toby I'm sorry, Adam. I promise this is not how I wanted this to go.

Morgan How *did* you want this to go?

Toby Well, obviously better than this!

Adam Just leave.

Toby Please don't go to South America with Tom.

Adam That is none of your business.

Toby Please don't choose him over me.

Adam This isn't about you, Toby.

Toby Yes it is because I love you!
  You know that Tom is a drug addict, right?

Adam Yeah, and you're a drunk.
  If you leave now, I promise I will never mention this
to Eric.

Toby Adam –

Adam But only if you leave right now.

Toby But . . . but it's raining.

  Adam grabs Toby's umbrella from Act One.

Adam Here. Take your shitty umbrella. I've been meaning
to give it back to you anyway.

Toby Adam –

Adam Goodnight, Toby.

Young Man 1 Adam picked up his phone to call Eric.

Morgan But he stopped himself before he could dial.

Young Man 1 Why would he do that?

Morgan That night in Chicago, when he told Toby the
story of what happened to him in Prague . . .

Young Man 1 He wanted to see how deeply he could
draw Toby to him. He was surprised at how well it
worked.

Morgan Perhaps it worked too well.

Young Man 1 Adam feared he might have been the
unwitting author of Eric and Toby's break-up.

Morgan And *that* was the thought that caused him to put down his phone. Adam may have triumphed over Toby . . .

Young Man 1 But at what cost to Eric?

End of Scene One.

SCENE TWO

Autumn 2016

Eric Autumn brought none of its usual joy to Eric Glass that year. He was forced to face the future alone.

Young Man 6 Toby had moved out a few days after their break-up.

Young Man 3 Walter was gone without a goodbye.

Young Man 4 Even Adam had vanished.

Young Man 5 And soon Eric's home would be gone, as well.

Young Man 7 Even his country was gone, having changed overnight like a sudden betrayal.

Eric Like Toby's betrayal.

Morgan Eric's plans for the future vanished overnight –

Eric – as if written in disappearing ink.

Young Man 8 Eric's first task was to find a new place to live.

Young Man 2 His next was to pack.

Eric He was daunted by both tasks.

Morgan And so it came as a great relief when Henry Wilcox knocked on Eric's door.

1. Eric's Apartment

Eric and Henry. Henry holds a crystal wine decanter.

Henry Is this a bad time?

Eric No, not at all. In fact, you're aiding and abetting in some very important procrastination. I've been thinking about you, actually.

Henry You have?

Eric Yes, and wondering how you've been.

Henry I'm fine, thank you. This decanter belonged to Walter. It was his grandmother's, actually. Waterford. Manufactured in the mid-nineteenth century.

Eric It's beautiful.

Henry I want you to have it.

Eric Oh no, Henry, I couldn't.

Henry You can and you will. You were a good friend to him, especially at the end.

Eric I didn't know it was the end.

Henry Which is what made it all the more genuine. Please take it.

Eric Henry, it's way too expensive.

Henry It would mean a great deal to me if you accepted this as a gift from me in gratitude for your kindness.

Eric For you, then. And for Walter's memory.

Henry Thank you.

Eric Thank *you*.

Henry Are you moving?

Eric Yes, unfortunately. End of the year.

Henry Why 'unfortunately'?

Eric I lost the lease here.

Henry You've been renting this place?

Eric I love that you and Walter both thought I was secretly rich.

Henry I didn't think it was a secret.

Eric I'm terminally middle class.

Henry Where are you going?

Eric *That* is a very good question. I'm honestly feeling a little overwhelmed right now.

Henry Where's Toby in all of this?

Eric Burning in hell for all I care.

Henry Oh.

Eric Toby and I broke up.

Henry I'm sorry to hear that, Eric. You're going through some things right now, aren't you?

Eric Not like what you've been through.

Henry It doesn't have to be a competition.

Eric I thought to businessmen, everything was a competition.

Henry Not when it comes to suffering.

Eric Are you suffering, Henry?

Henry I really wish I hadn't used that word.

Eric Yes, but you have, so it's in play. Are you suffering?

Henry develops a sudden interest in the floor.

Henry He still gets mail.

That's . . . well . . . and sometimes I'll forget he's . . . I'll think for a moment he's just in the next room and . . . anyway, I'm starting to realize just how much I depended on him.

Eric Funny. I'm starting to learn just how thoroughly undependable Toby was.

Henry I always liked the two of you together.

Eric Yeah, me too. But, you know, fuck him.

Have you been lonely since Walter . . . ?

Henry Work keeps me busy. And I have my sons.

Eric But are you lonely?

Henry I do listen to music now. I never did that before. Not in a maudlin way, just . . .

What's your plan, then? For the housing situation.

Eric The plan is to come up with a really good plan.

Henry Can you afford to buy?

Eric Maybe. If I look in the Bronx and it's 1977.

Henry All you have to do is fix your price, fix your neighborhood and don't budge. I could put you in touch with a broker, if you'd like.

Eric I would actually, thank you. I've had the wind taken out of me. And then the election. I'm still reeling from that, aren't you?

Henry Maybe not as much as you.

Eric It's actually a blessing that all of this is happening in the fall.

Henry Why is that?

Eric There's just so much to do in the fall: new movies, new plays, new books, dance, exhibitions. New York Film Festival, City Ballet. (Ooh, the new Justin Peck piece is coming up!) Restaurant Week, the BAM Next Wave Festival alone, my God! New York is the perfect place to waste your time and still maintain your dignity.

He notices Henry smiling.

What?

Henry I'd forgotten how vivid you are.

Eric Me? No I'm not, I'm just – what do you do for fun?

Henry I work.

Eric And when that gets old . . . ?

Henry It hasn't yet.

Eric Tell me one thing you do for fun.

Henry I read. History, mostly. Biographies, that sort of thing.

Eric Novels ever?

Henry Older ones. I find most contemporary fiction glib and self-conscious. Do you have plans tonight? I feel like having a nice dinner out. Do you want to come with me?

Eric Oh.
    I would love to.
    Oh shit, no!
    I have BAM tickets tonight.

Henry Ah. Another time, then.

Eric Yes.
    Actually, I have an extra ticket. What are your opinions on German expressionism?

Henry Oh. Well. I have no idea what that is but I'm pretty certain I hate it.

Eric How would you like to travel to Brooklyn with me tonight and broaden your horizons?

Henry Must they really stretch as far as Brooklyn?

Eric Boy, have you got a lot to learn, Henry Wilcox.

Henry And I suppose you think you're the person to teach me.

Eric About certain things, yes.

Henry How long is this thing at BAM?

Eric Four hours.

Henry My God, that's obscene.

Eric But there's two intermissions.

Henry All in German?

Eric *Ja.*

Henry Fine, but I reserve the right to renegotiate at the first intermission.

2. *Various Locations*

Young Man 3 Thus the tyranny of the autumnal New York cultural scene continued to hold its sway over Eric Glass, infecting Henry Wilcox as well with its unrelenting demands.

Young Man 4 Henry's life was entrenched completely in commerce. Yet in the weeks that followed, Henry spent more time inside theatres, museums and concert halls than he had in decades.

Henry What the fuck are we watching here?

Eric This playwright is a genius.

Henry Says who?

Eric Well, he won the MacArthur Award.

Henry Which means what, exactly?

Eric That he's a genius.

Henry But what makes him a genius?

Eric Beats me. I've never liked any of his plays.

Young Man 4 They frequented hot new restaurants in Bushwick that took no reservations and boasted of two-hour waits.

Young Man 3 Eric was appalled when Henry slipped the host a fifty-dollar bill. But his resistance faded when the action promptly landed them a table.

Henry Negotiation is like standing on opposing ends of a football field. The goal is to get the other guy to travel closer to your end of the field than you to his.

Eric You know that sports metaphors are completely lost on me, right?

Henry Decide what you want to hold onto but never let the other guy know what that is. Make him think everything is precious to you. That way he doesn't know what you're really willing to give up. Half of the things you ask for at the outset are there so you can make a show of letting go of them. And always be willing to walk away from the deal.

Morgan December arrived and Henry surprised both his sons by inviting Eric to join them for their annual visit to Peter Luger Steakhouse, the only reason Henry found a trip to Brooklyn was warranted.

3. Peter Luger Steak House

Eric, Henry, Charles and Paul at dinner.

Henry How is it you've lived in or around New York City all your life and you've never eaten here?

Eric It never occurred to me to travel outside of Manhattan for a steak. You can get a steak at any restaurant.

Paul No, you cannot.

Charles Not true at all.

Henry You can get grilled beef at any restaurant. But for a real steak, you have to come to Peter Luger's. What looks good to you?

Eric Everything. I can't decide.

Henry Let me order for the table, then. We'll start with the bacon. (Not on the menu – you have to know to order it.) Four shrimp cocktails. Then we'll have two orders of the Porterhouse for two, medium rare. Also the prime rib, medium rare.

Charles *and* **Paul** Yes!

Paul Peter Luger Sauce, please.

Henry *and* **Charles** Yes!

Henry What else? Baked potatoes?

Charles *and* **Paul** Yes!

Charles And steak fries.

Henry *and* **Paul** Yes!

Paul And the German hash browns.

Henry *and* **Charles** Yes!

Henry And for dessert, a piece of cheesecake and the Holy Cow sundae.

Charles *and* **Paul** Yes!

Henry Do we feel that's enough?

Eric Maybe a vegetable?

Paul We're getting three.

Henry I think he means something green. Creamed spinach?

Eric Yes!

Henry That's how you order at Peter Luger's.

Young Man 5 It quickly became apparent to Charles and Paul that their father was engaged in a kind of fucking courtship with Eric.

Young Man 2 The brothers sat dumbfounded as Henry prompted Eric to prattle on about whatever fucking subjects he could devise.

Henry How's the apartment hunt coming along?

Eric Ugh, it's not. I just got outbid by a cash offer. Twenty percent above asking. For a studio!

Henry This is why you need to have four or five other properties ready to make offers on next.

Eric I know, I know. I just loved that apartment so much.

Henry Eric, I have told you and told you: you can't be sentimental about real estate.

Eric I know, I know. I'm about to give up and start looking outside the city. Maybe you should just give me Walter's house.

Paul chokes on his drink.

Did I say something wrong?

Charles and Paul look at each other.

Don't tell me you sold it.

Paul You can't have it.

Charles It's rented.

Henry You don't want to live in the country, Eric. You're a city mouse through and through.

Eric I know. You're right. But it is tempting to think about leaving here. Well, if it ever becomes available, let me know. I'm at the point where I'm ready to throw in the towel and start raising alpacas.

Paul Alpacas?

Charles What the fuck?

4. *Elevator*

Eric Thank you so much for dinner tonight, Henry. It was nice to . . . Well, anyway, it was nice.

Henry It was my pleasure.

Eric Your sons think I'm a total weirdo.

Henry You *are* a total weirdo.

Eric I don't think they find it charming.

Henry I do.

Eric Do you ever worry about the future, Henry?

Henry No.

Eric How is that possible? Will you teach me?

Henry It's easy: just live through much worse and become a billionaire.

Eric Why didn't I think of that? It just feels as though the world is falling apart.

Henry The world has been falling apart since it began. That is what the world does: it falls, it's rebuilt. The same is true of people. You're stronger than you think.

The elevator dings.

Eric Do you want to come up to my place . . . for a bit?

Henry It's late. And I should be getting home.

Eric Yeah. Yeah, okay. Well. Goodnight, Henry.

Eric reaches his hand out and takes Henry's.

Thank you.

Henry Goodnight, Eric.

Henry exits.

Morgan Eric examined the decanter that Henry had brought him several weeks before.

Eric He thought about Walter and felt his loving embrace in that moment.

Morgan And in the next, longed for Henry's.

End of Scene Two.

SCENE THREE

Christmas Eve, 2016

Toby Toby rented a corner apartment on the 67th floor of a new construction in Hell's Kitchen. He bought clothes and furniture, he began working with a trainer –

Young Man 5 And started fucking his trainer.

129

Toby Toby was having the time of his life. Parties at the Public Hotel, dinners at the Polo Bar, threeways with Juilliard dancers.

Morgan But the emptiness he felt as a result of his break-up with Eric could not be easily pasted over by his libertine adventures.

Toby No, Toby was having fun.

Morgan But why was he having fun?

Toby Because he was young and handsome with a kick-ass fuck-pad in the heart of New York City.

Morgan Because he is in pain.

Toby What the fuck is Toby in pain about?

Morgan Take your pick: the end of his relationship with Eric, Adam's rejection, the critical indifference to his work. There's a 'why' behind every action. And very likely a 'why' behind every 'why'.

Toby (*ignoring him*) It was Toby and Eric's tradition to attend the matinee of *The Nutcracker* every Christmas Eve with Eric's friends.

Morgan But Toby was disinvited this year.

Toby Fine, then. It's a stupid ballet anyway. Toby thought of calling Adam.

Morgan But Adam was in Brazil with the director Tom Durrell.

Toby Fine, then. Toby called Tristan.

Tristan As if, bitch.

Toby Toby called the Jasons.

Jason 2 Oh my God, Toby!

Jason 1 Have you seen the new sonograms?

Jason 1 *and* **Jason 2** The baby is getting so big.

Toby Toby hung up on the Jasons.

Morgan Who then does Toby turn to?

Toby No one. Toby treats himself to a meal at Eleven Madison Park.

Young Man 3 Thanks for the tip. Merry Christmas!

Toby He goes home and . . . he goes home and opens an expensive bottle of wine.

Morgan And then what?

Toby He drinks it.

Morgan And then what?

Toby It tastes good.

Morgan And then what?
  Then he feels an overwhelming spasm of loneliness that, on this night, the wine could not alleviate.

Toby No.

Morgan And that is how he found himself online, seeking out less complicated companionship.

Toby Is Toby about to get laid? Totally down with that.

Morgan Toby was stopped short by the profile.
  Was it him?

Toby Who?

Morgan But no, it couldn't be.

Young Man 3 Who are you talking about, Morgan?

Morgan But that face. It was the same face, give or take.

Toby Whose face?

Young Man 3 Oh shit.

Morgan Toby knew he had to have this boy, if only for one night. If only to pretend. Toby texted the number on the ad and, two hours later –

Morgan turns to face Young Man 1.

Morgan – Leo appeared at his door.

1. Toby's Apartment

Toby Hi.

Leo Hey.

Toby Thanks for coming on such short notice.

Leo Yeah.

Toby Can I get you a drink?

Leo I'm good.

He goes to the window, staring out.

Toby Great view, huh? You can see the whole city.

Leo Cool.

He removes his hood, revealing his face.

Toby Holy shit.

Toby reaches for Leo. Leo pulls away.

Sorry, I – I've never done this before.

Leo With a guy?

Toby Oh God no. That ship has sailed. It's just my first time, you know . . .

Morgan Paying for it.

Toby So how does this work, exactly?

Leo You tell me what you want, I'll tell you if I do it.

Toby I wanna fuck you.

Leo Okay.

Toby How / much?

Leo looks around the apartment, and then decides:

Leo Three hundred.

Toby Okay.

Leo You have condoms?

Toby Oh. Ah –

Leo I brought some.

Toby I'm neg for what it's worth.

Leo Me too but I don't fuck raw.

Toby Right. I wasn't trying to not use them. I was just saying that you have nothing to fear from me. How old are you?

Leo Old enough.

He starts undressing. He then realizes Toby isn't.

Are you okay?

Toby Yeah. It's just that you're really beautiful, you know that? Can I kiss you?

Leo That's more intimate than I like.

Toby I'm about to fuck you.

Leo I know.

Toby But kissing is too intimate?

Leo Yes.

Toby I'll pay an extra hundred if you let me kiss you.

A beat.

Leo Okay.

Toby approaches Leo, takes a moment, then kisses him. Leo quickly pulls away. It's a two-dollar kiss at best. Leo continues undressing.

Toby What's your name?

Leo Leo.

Toby Can I call you 'Adam'?

Leo Why?

Toby You just look like an 'Adam' to me.

Leo Whatever, man.

Toby Will you . . . will you tell me you love me?

Leo What?

Toby I'll pay you another hundred.
Please.

Leo looks at Morgan for help.

Morgan Tell him.

Leo I love you.

Toby Say, 'I love you, Toby.'

Leo I love you, Toby.

Toby Say it again. Make me believe it.

Leo I love you, Toby.

Toby I love you, Adam. Again.

Leo I love you, Toby.

Toby I love you, Adam. Again.

Leo I love you, Toby.

A beat, then:

Toby Let's go to bed.

Lights shift then rise on Toby's bed. Toby is asleep.
Leo sits up, looking out Toby's massive windows. Both
are now naked.

Morgan Leo sat in Toby's bed, looking at the skyline
that – what?

Leo Shimmered?

Morgan Yes. That shimmered before him. He had never
been this high up in the city before. He couldn't help
being . . . what?

Leo Dazzled by the view.

Morgan Leo knew he should dress and go home, that the
trip would be a long one at this hour.

Leo He'd forgotten to ask for cash upfront.

Morgan Rookie mistake, not to be repeated.

Leo Leo would have to wake him to get his money. And
that got scary sometimes, even with the nice ones. The
need to ask made him feel . . . well, like a whore.

Morgan But sitting in this warm, comfortable bed,
looking out at the city, relaxed and even sleepy after his
unexpected orgasm –

Leo Leo took a breath and pretended for one, two, three
seconds that he belonged here, in this apartment, in this
man's bed.

Morgan The city was . . . hypnotic from way up here, safely above the chaos.

Leo From this great height, in this warm bed, for just this moment, Leo was safe.

Morgan For once, he could stare at the tiger –

Leo – and not fear its teeth.

Toby stirs awake.

Toby Did I fall asleep?

Leo Just for a minute.

Toby What are you doing?

Leo Getting dressed.

Toby What's the rush?

Leo It's late.

Toby Come here for a second.

Leo I should go.

Toby Stay.

Leo It's late.

Toby So stay.

Leo I can't. Really.
So, um . . .

Toby Yeah?

Morgan His money.

Toby Oh! Right, sorry. What's the damage?

Leo Five hundred.

Toby What?!

Morgan With the extras.

136

Toby Oh. Right.

Toby takes a wad of cash, hands it over.

Leo Thank you.

Toby Thank *you*.

He notices a small book in Leo's back pocket.

What book are you reading?

He snatches it.

Leo Please give that back to me.

Toby *The Open Road*. What's it about?

Leo Nothing. Give it back.

Toby It has to be about something.

Leo It's just a bunch of old poems about nature and shit.

Toby Read one to me.

Leo No.

Toby Oh go on. Read me one of your favorites. Please?
I'll pay you a hundred dollars to read me a poem right now.

Leo opens the book, looks for his favorite and reads.

Leo 'With lifted / feet –'

Toby Wait, that's the poem called?

Leo Oh. Um . . .
'Going Downhill on a Bicycle'.

Toby Okay, go on.

Leo 'With lifted feet hands still I am poised, and down the hill dart with heedful mind the air goes by in a wind –'
This is stupid, I can't do this.

Morgan helps Leo understand the verse.

Morgan
With lifted feet, hands still,
I am poised, and down the hill
Dart, with heedful mind;
The air goes by in a wind.

Leo
Swifter and yet more swift,
Till the heart, with a mighty lift,
Makes the lungs laugh, the throat cry
'O bird, see: see, bird: I fly!

'Is this, is this your joy,
O bird, then I, though a boy,
For a golden moment share
Your feathery life in air!'

Morgan Well done.

Toby Thank you.

He hands over a hundred-dollar bill.

Leo You're funny.

Toby Why do you say that?

Leo You act like we're friends.

Toby I make friends easily.

Leo I don't.

Toby So go.

Leo Yeah, okay.

Toby That wasn't me kicking you out.

Leo I was leaving anyway.

Toby I just want to make you feel comfortable here.

Leo You have.

Toby Can I see you again?

Leo Call me whenever you wanna fuck.

Toby Right. Yeah. Here . . . my card.

He pulls out a card, hands it to Leo.

Leo You have cards?

Toby Classy, no?

Morgan 'Toby Darling, Child of Privilege.'

Toby Keep it. In case you ever need me.

Leo Why would I need you?

Toby I don't know. Just in case you do.

Leo slides the card into his book, heads to the door.

You sure you don't want to stay over?

A moment, then Leo comes back into the room, approaches Toby and gives him a hundred-dollar kiss.

Leo Merry Christmas.

Leo exits.

End of Scene Three.

SCENE FOUR

December 2016

1. An Empty Apartment

Morgan Two days after Christmas, Henry attempted to solve Eric's housing dilemma.

Eric Oh wow!

Henry You like it?

Eric I love it!

Henry And it comes with a key.

Eric Well, I should hope so.

Henry No, numbskull. A key to the park.

Eric Gramercy Park?

Henry The one and only.

Eric I can't afford to buy this.

Henry The thing is that it's not for sale, it's just to rent. But you can afford it if you want it.

Eric How is that possible?

Henry Because I own it. What's the rent on your place right now?

Eric Five hundred and seventy-five dollars.

Henry Jesus, you've been getting away with murder. I'll charge you eight hundred.

Eric Henry, are you sure?

Henry Only if you commit to buying something next year.

Eric Deal! Thank you! My very own apartment off of Gramercy Park. I feel like a Henry James character.

He explores the apartment.

Henry I do have one other idea to run past you.

Eric You're just full of great ideas today.

Henry I'm going to be leaving for Paris just after the New Year.

Eric Oh. How long will you be gone?

Henry Possibly through the spring.

Eric Oh. I see. I'm . . . I'm actually sad to hear that.

Henry Yes, well . . . I was wondering . . . before we settle on this apartment . . .

Eric Yes?

Henry Why don't you come with me?

Eric To Paris?

Henry For the winter.

Eric Oh. Well . . . I have my work.

Henry I wasn't sure how much time you could afford to take off.

Eric I mean, I have vacation time, but not four months' worth.

Henry No. No, of course not.

Eric And besides, with the Inauguration coming up, I'm going to be really busy. We're running campaigns against the cabinet appointments, mobilizing protests –

Henry The thing is . . . these past few weeks, I've . . . I've grown very . . . I've gotten used to having you around and I don't see why that can't continue while I'm away.

Eric Jasper would kill me if I took time off right now.

Jasper Damned right I would.

Henry Jasper's world will spin without you, Eric. Mine perhaps will not. I'm going to miss you. And I don't want to. So why should I?

2. *Eric and Jasper*

Jasper What do you mean 'leave of absence?'

Eric I haven't taken a vacation in over a year.

Jasper And you're not getting one until we impeach this motherfucker or we vote him out of office. Vacations are canceled until at least the '18 midterms, don't you understand that?

Eric I have given you so much over the years. I'm asking you for two weeks for myself.

Jasper This isn't about me, Eric. It's about our country.

Eric My taking just a little time off is not going to make any difference. The world will spin without me.

Young Man 8 The next day, movers came to take Eric's things to his new place off Gramercy Park. What didn't fit went into storage.

Young Man 6 All that was left were Toby's possessions, which Eric had carefully boxed up, berating himself for doing Toby's work for him.

Young Man 2 And so, on New Year's Eve, the former partners met for their final goodbye.

3. *Eric and Toby's Apartment*

Toby sorts through a stack of books. Other moving boxes surround him.

Toby Why didn't I get a Kindle? I should have bought a Kindle. Of course, you can't take Kindles into the bathtub. But then again, you can't take *Infinite Jest* into the bathtub, either.

Eric You've never read *Infinite Jest*.

Toby Neither have you.

Eric Yes, but I don't tell people that I have.

Toby That was one time at a party and I was talking to Zadie Smith. She made me nervous. I lie when I'm nervous.

Eric You drink when you're nervous. You lie when you drink.

Toby Are you intentionally trying to pick a fight?

Eric Yes. You also left behind a box of your parents' things.

Toby looks at the box. After a moment:

Toby, I have plans I have to get to.

Toby You hate New Year's Eve. Where are you going?

Eric Henry invited me over.

Toby Henry? Why would anyone want to spend New Year's Eve with Henry Wilcox?

Eric I like Henry.

Toby What is there to like?

Eric I found enough in you to keep me occupied for seven years.

Toby continues to go through his books. Then:

I need you to know how sad this makes me.

Toby We were going to have to move out eventually.

Eric Not the apartment, Toby. Us. What happened to us?

Toby We just . . . we grew apart.

Eric But Toby, you haven't grown.

Toby Okay, you know what? Keep the books, I don't need them. Well this was a real nice clambake. See ya around.

Eric Aren't you going to take your parents' things?

Toby Toss 'em, I don't want them.

Eric I don't think you mean that.

Toby Trust me, I do. They did fuck-all for me while they were alive. I'm supposed to schlep their shit around for the rest of my life? Fuck 'em. I don't need what's in those boxes.

Eric You are setting the stage for one miserable life, Toby.

Toby Oh fuck you, Eric. At least I'm living my life. You'd have died of old age in this apartment if they hadn't taken it from you, eaten by your cats. Your whole life has been one safe move after another. So I don't want to hear from you / that I –

Eric Henry asked me to go to Paris with him.

Toby He did not.
  Did he?
  You're not seriously thinking of going, are you?

Eric Why shouldn't I go to Paris if I can?

Toby Are you fucking Henry?

Eric Are you fucking Adam?

Toby You bet your ass I am. It is the best sex of my life. You've never heard sounds like the kind that kid makes when I fuck him.

Eric Mazel tov, Toby. I'm so happy for you both. Maybe his parents can adopt you, too.

Toby Fuck you, Eric.

Toby turns to leave.

Eric Wait – please.

I love you, Toby. And the fact that you don't seem to understand how badly I'm hurting right now hurts me even more. Did you ever love me?

Toby Yeah, of course I did.

Eric seems to have an epiphany.

What?

Eric No one ever taught you what that means, did they?

Toby What the fuck are you talking about?

Eric Take these things your parents left behind.

Toby considers them a moment and then:

Toby No thanks.

Toby heads to the door. He turns and looks at Eric. After a beat:

See you around, then.

Morgan Why didn't Toby take his things?

Toby It's just old books.

Morgan Not the books. His parents' things. What is in there that scares Toby so much?

Toby Don't care. What happens next?

Morgan Nothing can happen next until you explore this question.

Toby Says who?

Morgan I say. If we are to learn what we mean to each other, we must first examine what we mean to *ourselves*. And we must be fearless and honest in that attempt –

Toby Yeah, I'm gonna call bullshit on that. Why should we listen to you lecture us about fearlessness and honesty? You were never honest about yourself in your lifetime.

The Lads jeer him.

Young Man 3 ⎱ Way out of line!
Young Man 5 ⎰ Unfair!

Toby Why is it unfair? He never once told the world who he was.

Young Man 1 We are telling this story today because the world knows who Morgan was.

Toby No, he left it for the world to discover after he died. But while he was alive, he was anything but fearless and honest. (*To Morgan.*) Isn't that right, Morgan? The great E. M. Forster, beloved by all the world. And secretly the gayest daisy in the field. (*To the Lads.*) E. M. Forster, whose two most famous words were 'only connect', could not do so himself. He didn't have sex until he was thirty-eight. He lived with his mother until she died. He locked himself in the closet all his life. (*To Morgan.*) You never told the truth about yourself so why the fuck should we listen to you now?

Morgan Because you now have the chance to be honest, which is something I was never given.

Toby You had countless opportunities to be honest. You lived until 1970. You watched the moon landing, for God's sake. You were alive during Stonewall. The world changed because people were brave. You weren't.

Young Man 1 Morgan wrote *Maurice* in 1912. That wasn't brave?

Toby No, because he hid it from the world for fifty-six years. (*To Morgan.*) Just imagine what would have happened if you had published a gay novel in your lifetime! You might have toppled mountains. You might have even saved lives. But you didn't do that. (*To the Lads.*) Morgan had his chance to be honest and he fucking squandered it. He left others to do the heavy lifting and then he slipped it in at the end. (*To Morgan.*) And because of that, you're fucking irrelevant. You're just books on a shelf gathering dust. You're a Merchant Ivory film.

Young Man 3 I like Merchant Ivory films.

Toby You have nothing to teach us because you can't possibly understand what it's like to live in freedom, to demand choices for yourself. Toby doesn't have to do anything he doesn't want to. He doesn't have to listen to you, he doesn't have to look in any boxes. Toby's gonna fuck who he wants and live how he likes because that is his right as a gay man in the world you did *nothing* to help build.

Toby exits.

Young Man 1 Morgan.

Silence.

Morgan You know, the thing is, lads: he isn't wrong.

The Lads protest.

He didn't say it as kindly as he could have. But he said it nonetheless: there's nothing I can teach you that you don't already know. You understand your story better than I could ever hope to.

He looks at them.

I think it would be best for me to leave you.

The Lads protest.

Young Man 4 Morgan, no. You are essential to our story.

Morgan No, lads. *You* are essential to your story. I like to believe I was helpful to you as you started it.

But I cannot help you finish it. It isn't my right to. The past must be faced. It must be learned from. But it cannot be revised. I had my time. Now it is yours.

The Lads protest.

Young Man 1 There's still so much you haven't told us. There's still so much we don't know.

Morgan You have everything you need. Trust in that. Trust in yourselves.

He then looks at them.

Oh, my lads, how I do love you. You have allowed me to see . . . what I could not live. What a gift! I think your lives are beautiful. And I know at what cost they have come. Tell your story bravely. It is a story worth telling. Take care of yourselves. Take care of each other. (*About Toby.*) Take care of him most especially.

I am certain we shall find each other again, by and by.

Morgan exits.
    They watch him depart a beat or two, then begin to look among themselves.
    Silence. A long, uncertain silence.

Eventually, we find ourselves back where we started: with the Young Men gathered together and Young Man 1 on the periphery of the group. Then, finally:

Young Man 1 He has a story to tell.

Young Man 8 It is banging around inside him, aching to come out.

Young Man 3 But how does he continue?

148

Young Man 4 He opens his favorite novel –

Young Man 5 – hoping to find inspiration –

Young Man 6 – hoping to find guidance from its author.

Young Man 2 But they are just words on a page –

Young Man 7 – written down a hundred years ago.

Eric And their author now refuses his summons.

Young Man 1 He must tell his story himself.

He sets down his copy of Howards End.

Young Man 1 Paris . . . in the wintertime . . . is . . . what?

Young Man 3 Cold.

Young Man 2 Grey?

Young Man 1 No. What else?

Young Man 4 Paris in the wintertime is . . .

Young Man 6 Paris in the wintertime is . . .

Young Man 8 Quiet.

Young Man 7 Simple?

Young Man 1 Not quite it.

Young Man 5 Paris in the wintertime is . . .

Young Man 1 Paris in the wintertime is . . . underrated.

Eric   Paris in the wintertime is *vastly* underrated.

Young Man 1 looks to the other Lads to gauge their reaction. They encourage him to continue.

Songs will never be written extolling its virtues. But Eric Glass found it enchanting.

Young Man 1 He visited Henry every weekend that winter.

Young Man 7 He skipped the Women's March.

Young Man 6 He missed the protests against the travel ban.

Young Man 4 But he did read Proust in the Tuileries and Hemingway in cafés.

Young Man 1 Eric and Henry grew closer, fonder.

Young Man 8 They traveled to St Tropez together when the weather warmed.

Eric America seethed and boiled but Eric's heart slowly healed.

Young Man 3 Henry Wilcox returned to New York in May, where his new West Village town house was finally ready to move into. Eric spent many evenings there.

End of Scene Four.

SCENE FIVE

Spring 2017

Young Man 5 One night in late May, Henry invited his sons over for dinner.

Young Man 2 They were chagrined when they arrived to discover that Eric was in the kitchen preparing the meal.

Young Man 3 But their resistance faded once they tasted his cooking.

Paul Not bad.

Charles Not bad.

Young Man 3 Deep into the meal's third bottle of wine, Paul unadvisedly opened his mouth.

Paul And on top of all the other bullshit I have to deal with, I've got this fucking tenant at Walter's house busting my balls about when he can get his deposit back.

Charles Paul, maybe tonight's not the –

Paul I'm like: I've got a three-hundred-million-dollar condo in Queens in the middle of construction – I don't have time to deal with this penny-ante bullshit.

Charles Paul.

Paul I don't know why you hang onto that house, Pop. You should just do us all a favor and sell the fucking thing.

Eric What's happening at Walter's house?

Paul Nothing for you to be concerned with. (*To Henry.*) They scorched the ceiling in the kitchen with a grease fire. They let their dog piss and shit all over the place. They almost killed the cherry tree by hitting it with a pickup truck.

Eric They damaged the cherry tree?

Paul This isn't your concern.

Eric Walter loved that tree. Has anyone gone up to look at it?

Paul It's a fucking tree.

Eric No, but to Walter that tree was . . . Henry, the cherry tree. With the pig's teeth suck in the trunk.

Paul Pig's teeth?

Eric I'm sorry. I know I'm overstepping.

Henry No, Eric. Don't apologize. What condition is the tree in, Charles?

Charles I don't entirely know. Apparently they took a chunk out of the side of it. I can send someone to go up and take a look.

Eric Henry, why don't you and I go? I'd love to see the house.

Charles Pop's very busy.

Paul Pop doesn't have time / to go up –

Henry Why do you want to see the house?

Eric Walter told me so much about it, I'd love to finally see it. And, ah . . . I do miss Walter.

Henry stares at Eric with a look that can only be described as adoration.

Henry I understand.

2. *Upstate New York*

Young Man 1 As you drive out of the city on certain roads, a miraculous thing happens. At a certain point where the Bronx meets Westchester, the city suddenly stops –

Eric – like a switch has been flipped –

Young Man 1 – and the country begins.

Young Man 3 The closer they got to the house, the less inclined Henry was toward conversation. Eric watched him tense with every mile, Henry's fingers tightly gripping the wheel.

Young Man 4 They drove up the last few miles in silence, eventually turning onto a state road, then a county road and then a meandering country lane. Eric's chest heaved with eager anticipation.

Young Man 3 It was late May and the trees were already lush with leaves, the countryside was young and fresh and expectant. Finally, when Eric felt he could stand the wait no longer, Henry slowed the car.

Eric Are we here?

Henry The property is just through those trees.

Eric Aren't we pulling in?

Henry The keys are at the caretaker's. It's just up the road.

Eric Oh, Henry, stop the car! I want to get out.

Henry Why?

Eric I want to explore.
Is that okay?

Henry It'll just be half an hour.

Eric But I'm here now.

A moment, then Henry smiles.

Henry Go on. I won't be long.

Eric stands alone for a moment. He breathes the air. The sound of birdsong can be faintly heard. It grows and increases its presence over time. Then the sound of a breeze rustling through the leaves of countless trees.

And then, ever so slowly, THE HOUSE BEGINS TO APPEAR, *like a great ship emerging through the mist, silently imposing its mystical presence upon us. Eventually it fills the stage, dwarfing Eric, clearly and insistently revealing itself to us. The house as Walter described it, as it has haunted Eric's imagination. We also see the grounds surrounding it. The cherry tree in front and the rolling meadow beyond. The color green is omnipresent: in the grass, in the trees, in the brilliant*

*morning sunlight diffusing itself through all the many
leaves. It is a wondrous sight.*
    As this is happening:

Eric The car turned away, and Eric stood by the hedgerow
that protected the property from the road and he stepped
for the first time onto the grounds. It was as if a curtain
had risen. It was exactly as Walter had described. The
meadow rolling down to the grove of trees. The air, filled
with breezes and birdsong. The cherry tree with the pig's
teeth stuck into the trunk, its branches covering the porch
with shade. The pink blossoms from earlier in the spring
still dancing around in the grass. He was struck by the
fertility of the soil; he had seldom been in a garden where
the flowers looked so healthy. Even the weeds were
intensely green. Why had the tenants fled from all this
beauty? For Eric had already decided that this place was
beautiful. And then, there before him was the house itself,
standing as it had for centuries. It wasn't at all what he
expected. In fact, he was momentarily disappointed.
It was old and simple – and yet altogether delightful. A
classic colonial-clapboard, painted white. Two red-brick
chimneys on either end. Eleven windows as you look up
from the front garden. To anyone else, it was simply a
house. But Eric knew it was Walter's house. And because
of that, it found it beautiful. Eric thought of Walter, and
the story of his friend Peter who came here to die, of all
the young men who came here to find peace in their final
days. He thought of all the men who died in those years
and what they might have become, what the world would
look like today had they been allowed to end their story
on their own terms. Eric wondered what his life would be
like if he had not been robbed of a generation of mentors,
of poets, of friends and, perhaps even lovers. Eric breathed
and filled his lungs with the past. It stretched before him
now, limitless – the past and the present, mingling together
inside this house, inside him.

Young Man 1 Eric approached the house.

Young Man 3 He laid his hand upon the door.

Young Man 6 It opened.

Young Man 2 The house was not locked up after all.

Young Man 4 Eric walked inside.

Young Man 5 Walter, is that you?

Eric No, I . . .

Young Man 5 I'm sorry. I thought you were Walter for a moment. You have his way of walking around the house.

Eric I'm Eric.

Young Man 5 Eric Glass?

Eric Yes, that's right. How did you –

Suddenly, the various rooms of the house start to fill with young men, each bathed in their own spectral light. The house is filled with ghosts.

Young Man 5 It's so nice to finally meet you. We've heard so much about you.

Eric Me? Who are you?

Young Man 5 I'm Peter.

Eric Peter?

Young Man 5 Peter West. I'm a friend of Walter's. Welcome home, Eric.

End of Part One.

Part Two

Act One

Spring 2017–Autumn 2017

SCENE ONE

1. Walter's House

Spring 2017. Eric exactly how we left him at the end of Part One. Except the ghosts have vanished. All that is left is Eric's astonished sense of them. And then –

Henry (*off*) Eric!

Eric I'm here, Henry.

Henry enters.

Henry Ah, you got in.

Eric The door was unlocked. / Henry, I –

Henry That figures. God, what a mess! Charles was right – the tree took a bad scrape. I'll need to call in an arborist. That tenant is definitely not getting his deposit back. (*Then:*) So. Is it what you thought it would be?

Eric I can't remember anymore.

Henry It's just an old house. With all the problems that come with one. The stairs need to be rebuilt. The furnace replaced. Probably a new roof soon enough.

Eric Henry, do you think it's possible this house is haunted?

Henry No.

Eric I mean, given all that's / happened here.

Henry This house is not haunted.

Eric It's just . . . I think I may have just seen a ghost.

Henry No, Eric – you did not see a ghost.

Eric I think I may have seen / several, in fact.

Henry That's just your imagination.

Eric But Henry, I promise you / I saw –

Henry There are no ghosts in this house, Eric. Just cold walls and low ceilings and barely any light in the winter. Listen, Eric . . .

Eric Do you look for the flaws in people the way you look for them in houses?

Henry Houses hide their flaws better than people.

Eric Do I have flaws?

Henry Oh good God, yes.

Eric What are my flaws, Henry?

Henry You can't take a compliment.

Eric I don't think that's true.

Henry You undervalue yourself.

Eric Isn't that the same thing?

Henry It's the reason for the thing.

Eric What else?

Henry You refuse to believe that you're beautiful.

This catches Eric.

Listen, Eric . . . I know how hard these last few months have been for you.

Eric You have no idea how much you've helped me.

Henry I think, in fact, I do. Because you've helped me just as much. And I've been thinking: what role can we play in each other's lives going forward?

Eric You've been thinking that?

Henry I think about you more than you know.
And . . . I wondered . . . if you would want to marry me.

A stunned silence.

My God, I've rendered Eric Glass speechless.

Eric You want to marry . . . me?

Henry Yes.

Eric But . . . why?

Henry You make me smile. Contrary to what most people think, I do like to smile.

Eric I think you have a very nice smile.

Henry I'm glad you think so because you've been the author of all my recent smiles.

A moment, then:

I want you in my life, Eric.

Eric I *am* in your life.

Henry I want you fully in it. I can provide you with the freedom to find meaning in your life. To become the man you're meant to be. All I ask is that you share your spirit with me.

Gentle, rolling thunder in the distance.

Eric Can I think about it?

If Henry's disappointed, he covers it up.

Henry Of course.

Eric It's just that it's a big decision and you caught me by surprise. / And Henry, I –

Henry You don't have to explain yourself, Eric.

Eric And I did see a ghost.

More thunder.

Henry We should probably head back.

Eric But we just got here.

Henry I saw what I needed to see.

Eric I was hoping we could spend the day here. Walter told me so much, but it feels –

Henry I'd like to beat the storm.

More thunder, this time louder. Eric looks at the house longingly.

Really, Eric, we should go.

Eric Yes. Yes, of course, Henry.

Henry I'll just lock up.

Eric exits. Henry stands there, a moment, looking at the house. He suddenly seems incapable of leaving. Then . . .
Young Man 3 and Young Man 4 enter.

Young Man 3 I can't see the house.

Young Man 4 Here, just behind these trees.
Oh wow! This isn't at all what I expected.

Young Man 3 It's smaller than I thought it'd be.

Young Man 4 Yeah, but just look at it! It's perfect. And look at that cherry tree – how beautiful! Just imagine the leaves in the autumn. And the blossoms each spring? Don't you think this place is beautiful? Oh and wow –

that meadow! Look at all those wildflowers. Come on! Let's go explore the property.

Young Man 3 We should probably wait here.

Young Man 4 I'll be right back.

Young Man 3 Don't go too far.

Henry Walter!

Young Man 4 runs off. Henry and Young Man 3 are alone. Young Man 3 looks at the property.

Young Man 3 It *is* beautiful, isn't it?

Young Man 4 comes running on, carrying a bundle of wildflowers in his hands.

Young Man 4 Look at these flowers. And there's an old barn. We could refurbish it, turn it into a dining pavilion. Won't that be something?
This is it, Henry. I feel it. Don't you feel it, too?

When he realizes no answer is forthcoming:

Are you sure this is what you want?

Young Man 3 I want to live.

Young Man 4 shows Young Man 3 his bouquet. Young Man 3 sneezes.

Young Man 4 You'll get used to it.

Henry sneezes.

Eric Henry!

Henry Coming, Eric.

Young Man 4 And so Henry Wilcox locked the door to Walter's house and walked away from it, determined that he would never see it again.

End of Scene One.

Summer 2017

Young Man 6 Eric Glass had a decision to make.

Young Man 2 It was clear Henry's offer was sincere –

Young Man 6 – and Eric knew his answer had to be as well.

Young Man 5 He attempted to understand their relationship in a way he could explain to himself and his friends.

Young Man 8 And so Eric decided to introduce Henry to his friends.

Young Man 6 He planned one of his famous Sunday brunches in Henry's sumptuous new West Village townhouse –

Young Man 8 – privately fretting that Henry might not do well under the glare of their careful inspection.

Young Man 7 And so when Jasper asked if he could bring his new boyfriend –

Young Man 3 Tucker!

Young Man 7 – Eric happily agreed.

Young Man 2 They arrived an hour late.

1. Henry and Eric's Townhouse

Eric, Henry, Tristan, Jasper, Jason 1, Jason 2 and a new face, Tucker, Jasper's new boyfriend.

Jasper We met at Cochella. Tucker's an artist. He makes the most incredible . . . tell them what you call it.

Tucker Faux-art.

Tristan What is 'faux-art'?

Jason 2 Like out of Vietnamese noodles?

Tucker False art.

Tristan Meaning what?

Tucker Meaning that it isn't real.

Eric Like an illusion?

Tucker You could say that.

Jason 2 Like David Copperfield?

Jasper It's real in the sense you can see it, touch it.

Tristan Are we talking sculpture? Paintings?

Tucker Paintings.

Eric (*attempting to understand*) False paintings.

Tucker Yes.

Tristan But what makes them false?

Jasper Ah! Here's the genius part. Tell them.

Tucker You can tell them. They're your friends.

Jasper Yes, but it's your art. You should tell them.

Tucker I want to hear you describe it. It turns me on.

Tristan Oh for fuck's sake, just tell us!

Jasper It's false because he doesn't mean it.

    A beat, then.

Eric What do you mean, 'He doesn't mean it'?

Jasper They're false.

Tristan You've lost me.

Jasper Okay here: take a look at Tucker's Instagram.

Tucker hands the Jasons his phone.

Jason 1 But these are beautiful.

Jason 2 Look at that one.

Henry Let's have a look.

They hand the phone to Henry. Eric moves over to him, looking over his shoulder. The Lads take note of this intimacy.

You painted this?

Tucker Which one are you looking at?

Henry This landscape.

Tucker Yeah, I did that last week.

Henry And this portrait . . . ?

Tucker My grandmother.

Henry You're a Rembrandt, kid. The shading, the depth of color.

They get to one that's –

Eric Whoa!

Henry Is that you, Jasper?

Tristan ⎱ Jasper?
Jason 2 ⎰ There's a portrait of Jasper?

Eric Not a portrait.

Henry A nude.

Tristan What?

Jason 1 ⎱ You're kidding.
Jason 2 ⎰ Let me see.

They all gather around Henry.

Jason 1] That's . . .

Jason 2] Oh my.

Tristan Your dick isn't that big.

Young Man 7 *and* **Young Man 8** Yes it is.

Eric Who's your gallerist?

Jasper Tucker doesn't sell them.

Jason 1 Why not?

Tucker Because they're false.

Tristan BUT WHAT DOES THAT MEAN??

Tucker It means that they mean nothing to me. I can dash them off in an afternoon.

Tristan Bullshit.

Eric Those are . . . You're a . . .

Henry I think I know what word is coming.

Eric I'll say it anyway: a genius.

Jasper He is.

Tucker No, I'm not a genius. But I am brilliant.

Henry So what do you do with the canvases?

Tucker I burn them.

Jason 1 You're kidding.

Tristan Stop.

Eric You burn these?

Jason 2 Why?

Tucker They don't reflect how I see the world. I just . . . make them.

167

Eric But they're beautiful.

Tucker Beautiful but meaningless.

Eric Now wait . . . you cannot tell me there is no meaning in this portrait of your grandmother. Her eyes are so soulful, her face so kind. How is that untrue?

Tucker Because my grandmother's a fucking cunt, dude.

Jasper False art!

Tristan So all of your paintings are . . .

Tucker The world as you would like me to show it to you.

Tristan I *knew* Jasper's dick wasn't that big.

Eric A lot of people would buy these paintings.

Jasper Which is exactly why he destroys them.

Henry So you paint these paintings, these . . . well hell, I'll say it: these masterpieces.

Eric Wow, Henry.

Henry But you don't mean them. You can just dash them off, like Mozart scratching out the symphony he hears in his head. And then you destroy them.

Tucker Exactly.

Henry Because they're false.

Tucker Because they're false.

Henry So here's my question . . .

Tucker Lay it on me, Daddy-O.

Henry Why take a picture? If what you paint is false, if you don't stand behind its meaning, and the only reason for its creation is its destruction . . . why take a picture?

Tucker To show the world what is false and what is true.

Henry Why not just paint what is true?

Tucker Because no one wants the truth anymore.

Eric People are desperate for the truth.

Tucker People want the illusion of truth. They want a story that validates their beliefs: about themselves, their nation, the world.

Henry 'When the legend becomes fact, print the legend.'

Eric *Man Who Shot Liberty Valance*!

Henry Gold star!

Eric Henry's been showing me old John Ford movies.

Henry I want to go back to this picture idea because you haven't really convinced me. Why do you take a picture before you destroy it? I think it's because you want the credit for having made it without taking responsibility for what it means.

Tucker It means nothing. It's just beautiful.

Eric But beauty has tremendous meaning.

Tucker Only if it's true.

Henry How is a Schubert string quartet 'true'? Or a Frank Lloyd Wright design? That portrait of your grandmother may not be 'true' but it certainly is beautiful and / in painting it –

Tucker That's not who / she is, though.

Henry Let me finish, Tucker. And in painting it, you've taken something that is ugly to you and you've made it beautiful. If that doesn't demonstrate the genuine power of art, I don't know what does. I don't think you mistrust beauty, Tucker. I think you mistrust the truth. I think you mistrust yourself.

Tucker Hot!

Eric The conversation continued as Eric went to the kitchen to make coffee. He lingered by the door and watched as Henry engaged his friends about their lives, their work, their passions. Henry seemed invigorated to be among them. In that moment, Eric glimpsed the future that was opening to him. But as he returned with the cookies –

Jason 1 Wait, wait, wait! You're a Republican?

Jasper Eric, did you know about this?

Eric Well, I mean . . . I knew that Henry was relatively conservative, / but –

Jasper And that he gave money to the party last year, including to the nominee?

Eric You donated to his campaign?

Henry I did.

Eric Why?

Henry He asked.

Tristan You know him?

Henry Of course I do.

Eric And you gave him money?

Henry I'm a Republican. This can't be such a surprise.

Eric Well, I figured you were –

Henry A 'good' Republican?

Eric Well . . . yes.

Henry I *am* a good Republican. I gave money to the nominee. As I do every four years.

Jason 1 Why are you a Republican, Henry?

Henry Lots of reasons. I'm a businessman. I believe in low taxes, free markets. Why shouldn't I be a Republican?

Jason 2 Hello Mary, you're gay!

Henry Being gay can't be all you care about when you vote, is it, Jason?

Jason 2 It's one of the more important things to me.

Henry Why are you entitled to vote your self-interest and I'm not entitled to vote mine?

Jason 2 Because I'm a good person! And my self-interest ultimately benefits the nation.

Henry Yes! Spoken like a true liberal. I like to believe that I'm a good person and I also happen to believe that my self-interest benefits the nation. The difference is you define your self-interest based on your sexuality and I don't.

Jasper Because you can afford not to.

Eric So I discovered this bakery on the Lower East Side –

Jason 1 So how do you define your own self-interest, Henry? As a gay billionaire Republican? Besides giving him money, did you actually vote for him?

Henry Yes.

Jason 1 But why?

Henry I vote what's good for the market.

Jasper Is that all you care about?

Henry I didn't say that, Jasper. But it is what I base my vote on.

Jason 1 But what about the Republicans' age-old hostility to the LGBT community?

Henry Compared to the minutes-old embrace by the Democrats?

Tristan Or the Reagan administration's willful inaction during the epidemic?

Henry I bet you can't guess which US president was the first to make meaningful progress toward attempting to stem the spread of HIV in sub-Saharan Africa?

Jason 2 Bill Clinton.

Henry George W. Bush, your former favorite bogeyman.

Jasper Yes, but PEPFAR was aimed at the straight epidemic, not the gay one, and it didn't stop him from promoting anti-gay marriage bills in eleven states / as a strategy to –

Eric So Tucker, when you burn the paintings, is it like a kind of ritual?

Tucker I'm completely naked when I do it. Sometimes I cum afterward.

Tristan You're not actually suggesting that Republicans have done more to fight the spread of HIV than Democrats, are you?

Henry I'll throw a real curveball at you, Tristan. The story of the epidemic is usually told as a triumph of activism and direct action. But it can also be told as a triumph of free market principles – and of innovation.

Tristan Please Henry, do pitch that ball.

Henry When the epidemic began, we knew absolutely nothing about the virus, including the fact that it was a virus. And, within a period of roughly thirteen years, we had identified it, learned its pathology and begun successful drug treatments to greatly halt its spread.

You'd have to look at the Manhattan Project to find a faster timeline. And how was it accomplished? It –

Jasper It was accomplished because activists / fought for –

Henry Forgive me Jasper, that was a rhetorical question – it was accomplished because scientists and pharmaceutical companies / took the initiative despite intransigent gridlock within the FDA.

Jasper Pharmaceutical companies! (*After 'FDA'.*) It was the activists who pressured the FDA to relax standards to fast-track drugs.

Henry ⎱ Yes, Jasper. I know this.

Eric ⎰ Jasper, let him speak.

Jasper Clinical trials happened at record speed / because of the work of those activists.

Henry If you'd let me finish my sentence, Jasper, you would have heard me say that very thing. We are, believe it or not, in agreement on that. What that did was it unleashed the drug companies to begin innovating in ways they'd never been allowed to. The activists, whether they realized it or not, employed libertarian principles in order to free the drug companies from onerous government oversight, which allowed them to –

Jasper The drug companies were forced into action / by activists.

Henry No, they were *driven* into action by profit motivation, which in turn led to market innovation, which ultimately led to the introduction of drug cocktails and, a mere twenty years after the start of the epidemic – to Truvada. We went from absolute ignorance to reliable treatment and the prevention of transmission within twenty years! Those drug companies, like all companies, wanted to make a buck. And in doing so, they ended up saving tens of millions of lives.

Tristan Yeah, but that's only half of the infected population. And it ignores the fact that if you're a gay black man in America, your chances of contracting HIV are one in two. When we talk about the epidemic being over, we only mean among middle-class white men.

Henry Tristan, my God – one in two?

Tristan You won't read about *that* in the *Wall Street Journal*.

Jason 2 You know, I don't think gay people should have to pay taxes.

All eyes on Jason 2.

Henry You don't, huh?

Jason 2 NO!! Why the fuck should I pay taxes to a government that wants to deny me all my rights?

Eric Yes! Or African-Americans, for that matter.

Tristan I should get a double rebate for that.

Jason 2 Yes! Walk into your accountant's office, 'Oh yes, I'll take two oppression exemptions, please.' Same for women, transfolk, immigrants. Oh! Better still, we should be able to choose where our money goes when we pay our taxes every year. Like a whole list of boxes we get to check. They could make it look like a Dim Sum menu, you know? 'Let's see – we'll pay for education, the arts, and lemme have some of that equal protection under the law . . .'

Jason 1 Yes! I'll pay for Ruth Ginsburg's salary but not Clarence Thomas.

Jason 2 Yes! And there should be a comments section when you pay your taxes. 'Dear Mr Government – you may not spend my tax money on war, discrimination or to build any motherfucking walls.'

Henry Aha! Jason – I hate to break this to you, but that was spoken like a true libertarian!

Jason 2 I'm vers, baby.

Henry Ultimately what we're talking about here is a difference in philosophy.

Jasper No, what we're talking about here is a difference in morality.

Eric I think what we're discussing is the divide between the responsibility to community and the responsibility to the self, are we not? I mean, I do think it's possible to effect real change in the world by concentrating on the personal sphere and letting the global sphere take care of itself.

Jasper 'Let the global sphere take care of itself'? Have you been reading Ayn Rand in addition to watching old westerns?

Eric No, I'm just trying to find a link between what you're saying, Jasper, and what Henry is saying.

Jasper There is no link.

Eric There has to be. As a kid, I used to stare at the map of the United States in class. And I always thought that America was kinda shaped like an animal in a way. Maine is the head and Florida is the front legs.

Tucker What are the back legs?

Eric Well, it doesn't really have back legs. I was seven. Anyway – it's always caused me to think of America as a living, breathing organism, which we can then break down all the way to its cellular level, which is its citizenry. The Constitution starts with the word 'we'. 'We the People . . .' It's there, written into our DNA.

Henry God, I love how you think. Heal the cells and the body will become healthy. It's a principle that works in biology and in politics. It is also – correct me if I'm wrong, Tristan – exactly how HIV is treated.

Tristan You may not know this, Henry, but I'm not just a physician, I've also been living with HIV for fifteen years. Your analogy is apt but you could take it even further if you wanted.

Henry Please.

Tristan Everyone remember Bio 101? 'How the Immune System Works'?

Tucker I don't.

Tristan So you've got your T-cells, right?

Tucker What are T-cells?

Tristan It's like on *Game of Thrones*.

Tucker Oh.

Tristan And the T-cells are like the Night's Watch.

Tucker Oh!

Tristan They buzz around the bloodstream, looking for trouble, sounding the alarm at the first sign of infection.

Tucker Calling for Daenerys Targaryen and her dragons!

Tristan Yes. Now unlike most other viruses, which attach themselves to any number of human cells, HIV attaches itself exclusively to the T-cells, the very cells that are meant to be guarding against such infections.

Tucker Oh, like the White Walkers breaching the Wall!

Tristan Exactly. Now with the T-cells compromised, the body's autoimmune system shuts down. So if America is an organism and its citizenry is its cells, then what are its T-cells? What constitutes the American Immune System?

Tucker Jon Snow!

Jason 1 Journalism!

Jasper Activism!

Jason 2 Politics!

Eric Voting!

Tristan Yes! But Henry – if America is an organism and if its T-cells are its democracy, then what about that man you gave money to? Where does he fit in this analogy? You could say he is HIV: a cunning, pernicious retrovirus that has attached himself to the very core of American democracy and is now destroying the American Immune System: journalism, activism, politics, and even voting. And, like HIV, he is replicating his genetic material from tweet to tweet, from person to person, institution to institution, across the entire nation. Consequently, America is now falling prey to opportunistic infections its immune system had once been able to fight: fear, propaganda, sexism, homophobia, transphobia, white nationalism. And so, like any person with untreated HIV, you could say this nation has developed the American Immune Deficiency Syndrome. Let's just call it what it is and diagnose it properly: America. Has. AIDS.

Henry Tristan, you are brilliant! Come work for me. I want to pay you to think for a living.

Tristan Oh Henry, you can't afford me.

Eric Okay, I think we've had enough politics for one afternoon. Would anyone like some cake?

Tucker I'd love some, thanks!

Jasper How much money do you make a year, Henry?

Eric Jasper! You do not need to answer that, Henry.

Henry I don't mind, for the sake of debate. It's hard to answer too accurately.

Jasper Ballpark it.

Henry Let's say a quarter of a billion dollars a year.

Tucker Wow. That's a lot of money.

Eric There, Jasper: you have your answer. Who wants coffee and cake?

Jasper Do you think you might care a little more about what happens to powerless people in this country if you weren't a wealthy white, privileged male?

Henry I wasn't born wealthy, Jasper. And certainly not privileged. Although I confess you do have me on white. My father was a car mechanic and my mother was an elementary school teacher. What did your parents do for a living?

Jasper There's a difference between being born to the white working class in the 1950s and being born into poverty now. Economic inequality is expanding in this country at an exponential rate.

Henry What do you propose I should do about that?

Jasper Pay more taxes! The Constitution starts with 'We the people,' not 'We the people who have good accountants.'

Henry Okay, let's pretend for the sake of argument that I were to give all my surplus money away and give it to the poor. Let's pretend that every American does – yourself included. Who gets it? Is everyone included in this scheme or only the pure of heart?

Jasper I wouldn't place an ideological litmus test on it.

Henry So you're willing to make sacrifices even for a rural white Southern bigot who hates every single one

of us in this room but who is just as much in need of
economic assistance as the United Colors of Benetton
ad you most likely see in your head when you think so
romantically of the poor? When you say 'we the people',
Jasper, do you really mean that? Or do you mean 'we the
people who agree with me'?

Jasper We could start with the people who have lost their
homes so you can build your high rise condos all over
the city.

Eric Jasper, / come on.

Jasper Or to the homeless people living in the condemned
buildings you routinely grab up for pennies on the dollar.

Henry Jasper, it isn't my responsibility as a real estate
developer to end homelessness. Nor is it my job as a
billionaire to fix income inequality.

Jasper No, it's your responsibility as a human being.

Henry I am responsible to my family, to my employees,
my investors. If homelessness, if income inequality is
your passion, then it should be your fight. You and I have
different philosophies and therefore different priorities.
Just because I don't share yours doesn't make me a villain.
No one opened any doors for me nor did me any favors.

Jasper What you're ignoring is that, while you may have
had humble beginnings, you have been on a glide path to
success from the day you were born because you're a
white male in America and because of that, doors were in
fact open to you that have been resolutely sealed to so
many other people in this country.

Eric Jasper –

Jasper You don't give a fuck about our community or
this nation because for a man like you, being gay is just
a speed bump on your journey. You've arrived at your

station in life without ever once understanding suffering or the meaning of adversity.

Henry I pray, Jasper, that you never learn the true meaning of adversity. I pray that you never know what it is like to live in fear for your life. I sincerely hope you're forever shielded from misfortune. But you see, my boy, I wasn't. No one saved me. I saved myself. Whether you realize it or not, whether you like it or not, you are the man you are today because men my age paid for your rights with their lives.

Jasper I didn't mean that gay men your age / didn't –

Henry THERE ARE NO GAY MEN MY AGE.
Not nearly enough.

A moment, then:

Gentlemen, it has been an enjoyable if pugnacious afternoon. A pleasure to meet you all.

Eric Henry, don't go.

Henry I'll be upstairs if you need me. I have some calls to return. Tucker, if you ever want to sell me one of your paintings, I promise I'll never look at it.

He exits. Seething silence, then:

Eric Jasper, I don't even know what to say to you right now.

Jasper You don't know what to say to *me*? Eric . . . Do you see the person you're mixed up with?

Eric That 'person' has a name. He also has a home and you are inside it. I noticed you didn't have a problem with him while you were eating his food and drinking his wine.

Jasper I was trying to be polite!

Eric You searched his political contributions online and then threw it in his face.

Jason 2 You were pretty nasty about it, Jasper.

Jasper Guys, he is part of the problem.

Eric So then leave his fucking house.

Jasper Eric . . .

Jason 1 He didn't mean that, Jasper / he's just –

Eric I don't need you to speak for me, Jason.

Jasper I can't believe you're defending him.

Eric I can't believe that you're making me. I invited you here to meet Henry because he's become very important to me. But if you feel so strongly about it, Jasper, then you shouldn't have come and you definitely should leave.

Jasper Fine. Come on, Tucker.

Tucker But there's cake still.

Jasper Look, Eric, I know you've been through a lot / this past year or so –

Eric Don't pretend to be concerned for me. This has nothing to do with me, / Jasper.

Jasper It has *everything* to do with you. You've become a billionaire Republican's kept boy.

Eric Henry asked me to marry him.

Stunned silence from the Lads.

Jasper You're not actually thinking about it, are you?

Eric I don't have to explain myself to you.

Tristan Actually, Eric, I think you do.

Eric Oh come on, Tristan, you too?

Tristan Eric, this is enormous. And we are all your closest friends. We have a right to know your mind.

Eric acquiesces with silence.

So tell me: are you asking for our opinion or for our blessing?

Eric I don't know. Both, I guess. Except from Jasper.

Tristan Do you love Henry?

Eric In a way, yes.

Tristan 'In a way'?

Jason 1 Is that enough, Eric?

Jason 2 Are you two fucking?

Eric We haven't yet.

Tristan So what is Henry offering you that you believe you need?

Jasper Besides a billion dollars.

Eric He's offering me happiness and comfort and peace. Why shouldn't I want that?

Jasper Because you'd be throwing away your life, Eric.

Tristan Ignore Jasper.

Jasper No, don't ignore Jasper!

Tristan I'm not saying this because I don't want you to be happy. I'm saying it because I don't want you to be hurt. I'm talking right now about your gorgeous, compassionate heart. Will Henry care for that?

Eric He already does!

Tristan You and Henry are very different people. He's prose and you're poetry.

Jason 1 He's logic and you're passion.

Jasper He's evil and you're not.

Eric STOP ATTACKING HIM, JASPER! So he doesn't agree with you on politics. That doesn't mean he isn't a good person.

Jasper Google Henry's company sometime. Read about the things he's done.

Eric Henry listens to me and makes me feel valued. Toby used me and discarded me. Where were your doomsday predictions when I first met Toby?

Jasper Toby's a vain, self-destructive narcissist. But at least his heart's in the right place.

Eric I cannot ask you to like Henry. But goddamnit, Jasper, you will respect him. Because he deserves your respect.

Jasper What makes him so deserving of my respect?

Eric The fact that he's won mine.

Jasper Eric, if you marry this man, don't expect me to come to the wedding. And don't expect your job to be waiting for you when you come back from your honeymoon.

Jason 1 Jasper, come on.

Eric You would end our friendship over this?

Jasper We are fighting for our nation's soul. For its very survival. I do not have room in my life for anyone who doesn't agree with that basic truth.

Eric Jasper, this is my life.

Jasper And this is my country.

2. *Henry's Study*

Henry at his desk. Eric enters.

Eric Henry, I'm so sorry about all that.

Henry Don't be. I like your friends. And they seem to care very much about you.

Eric I've been thinking about your proposal, Henry.

Henry Come to any decisions?

Eric I would like to marry you. I would *love* to marry you. If you'll still have me.

Henry I would have waited a lot longer than that. Good. Good!

Eric smiles. They both smile.

Eric Should we set a date, or –?

Henry I need to talk to my sons first.

Eric Yes, of course.

Henry Once that's done, I'll call a friend of mine who's a Federal judge and we can get married right away.

Eric Actually, I was hoping we could have the teeny tiniest of parties. We don't even have to call it a wedding. We can call it, um, a 'celebration of marriage'. We can do it at your farm in Dutchess County. In the fall when the leaves are changing. I promise no more than thirty people.

Henry Yes. Let's have a small, intimate, very expensive 'celebration of marriage.'

Eric Can we have, like, three different cakes?

Henry Let's have a dozen.

Eric Could I have a new suit made?

Henry Of course. One thing: you don't have to ask permission to spend my money.

Eric That's going to take me a little while to get used to.

Henry Once you *do* get used to it, that's when you should definitely start asking permission.

Eric Deal. Holy shit, we're engaged.

Henry Holy shit, we are.

Eric Should I spend the night?

Henry Tonight's not the best for me. And you're far too distracting.

Eric Well . . . before I go . . . I was thinking . . . maybe you should fuck me.
    Because I really want you to. I am at six thousand on the horniness scale.

Henry Sex isn't really what I'm after.

Eric I understand. It's been a long day. And we've got plenty of time.

Henry Sex has never been that important to me.

Eric Are you attracted to me, Henry?

Henry Yes. Yes, of course.

Eric So . . . will we eventually have sex?

Henry That's not . . . why I want you.
    I don't care what you do outside of the marriage. All I ask from you is tact and discretion.

Eric How can a man as vital as you not be interested in sex?

Henry I've learned to concentrate on other things. I hope that isn't a deal-breaker for you.

Eric Well, it's . . . certainly a bombshell. Will we share a bed?

Henry If you like.

Eric I'm going to sleep next to you but not get fucked by you?

Henry I wish you'd stop thinking in such absolutes. You should move in as soon as possible.

Eric Should I bring all my things?

Henry Your things?

Eric My grandmother's furniture.

Henry I have all the furniture I need.

Eric But they're Grandmother's things.

Henry We can store them upstate.

Eric At Walter's house?

Henry It's just sitting there empty. All that matters to me is that you move in as soon as possible. This house gets too quiet without you.

Eric Okay. Thank you, Henry.

Henry goes back to work. Eric leaves.

Henry Walter.

Young Man 4 Yes, Henry?

Young Man 3 Walter, take your clothes off.

Henry He's reading.

Young Man 3 What are you reading now?

Young Man 4 *Maurice*.

Henry His favorite.

Young Man 3 You've read that already. Take your clothes off now. I wanna fuck you.

Young Man 4 But we've already fucked today.

Young Man 3 I wanna fuck you again.

Young Man 4 And again and again / and again?

Henry And again.

Young Man 3 Why not? Let's never stop.

Young Man 4 Why do you want to fuck me, Henry?

Young Man 3 I love the sounds that you make when I do.

Young Man 4 You make me make them.

Young Man 3 Let me hear them again.

End of Scene Two.

SCENE THREE

Summer 2017

Toby enters.

Toby Hey, boys – miss me?

The Lads catcall and cheer his entrance.

Young Man 6 Where've you been, motherfucker?

Toby Patiently awaiting my re-entrance into the story. So – Toby Darling.

Young Man 2 Lay it on us, baby.

Toby One may as well begin with Toby's phone call to his agent. (*To Young Man 5.*) I've started working on a new play.

Young Man 5 becomes Toby's Agent.

Agent Fantastic! What's it about?

Toby Oh, it's gonna be terrific! Filled with themes and ideas.

Agent Yeah?

Toby Characters and plot.

Agent Wow.

Toby Dialogue and punctuation.

Agent You don't have any ideas for a new play, do you?

Toby Nope, not a thing. Fuck it. Toby doesn't feel like working right now. His play is going to Broadway in the fall.

Young Man 3 So what's he been up to?

Toby Happy you asked! One may as well begin with Toby's love life. Toby has started dating this really hot guy.

Young Man 8 Toby, I want you to meet my parents!

Toby You know, on second thought, Toby doesn't want to get tied down with anyone right now. Toby's doing just fine on his own.

Young Man 2 That's great, Toby.

Toby Yeah!
So.
One may as well begin with Toby's . . .
How's Eric doing?

Young Man 3 Eric? He's terrific! In fact / he just got –

Toby You know what? Fuck it, I don't care.

Young Man 7 Has Toby talked to Adam recently?

Toby Nah, Toby hates hanging out with actors. All they

wanna do is talk about themselves. Toby, on the other hand / has been spending lots of time in LA, building up his film career.

Leo Excuse me? I'm sorry, excuse me?

Toby Drinks at Doheney Room. Dinners at Factory Kitchen.

Leo Excuse me? I'm sorry to bother you.

Toby What?! I'm in the middle of –
Adam? What the fuck are you doing here?

Leo Adam? No, I'm Leo.

Toby Leo?

Leo We met last Christmas?

Toby What? Like at a party, or – ?

Leo No, here. We –

Young Man 8 The kid with the book.

Toby Oh right! Why are you here? Did I text you last night? I don't really remember what I –

Leo That night we met, you gave me –

Toby Oh – wasn't me, baby. I get tested regularly.

Leo You gave me your card, remember?

Young Man 8 'Toby Darling, Child of Privilege'.

Leo You told me to reach out if I needed anything.

Toby I did?
That was very nice of me.
So . . . what do you need?

Leo Kindness?

Young Man 6 But what Leo actually said was:

Leo Can I take a shower?

Toby A shower?

Leo And wash my clothes?

Toby You knocked on my door at eight in the morning to ask if you could do laundry?

Leo nods.

Toby Can't you just . . . do it at home?

Leo Forget it, I'm sorry.

Young Man 6 And then Toby looked at Leo's clothes.

Young Man 8 Rank and dirty.

Young Man 5 Hair greasy.

Young Man 3 Leo smelled.

Young Man 4 And Toby said:

Toby I mean . . . I guess if you really need to –

Leo Thank you.

Toby gets a laundry bag.

Toby Well? Hop to it, kid. Strip.

Leo starts undressing.

Where do you live, Leo?

Leo Around.

Toby What does that mean?

Leo Just . . . You know . . .

Toby Do you not know where you live?

Toby catches Leo retreating into himself.

Oh.

Are you . . . I don't know what we're supposed to say anymore. Are you experiencing homelessness right now?

Leo does not answer.

Toby How old are you?

Leo Nineteen.

Toby I'll get the shower started for you.

Young Man 2 Toby starts the shower.

Young Man 5 And he instantly feels the burden of Leo's need.

Young Man 8 Toby likes to be wanted but he hates to be needed.

Young Man 7 But as he catches sight of Leo standing there in his living room, Toby remembers why he had chosen him that night:

Toby Leo's striking resemblance to Adam.

Young Man 2 But, staring at Leo, Toby realizes how different he and Adam are.

Young Man 4 Toby is reminded of how easily he could have shared this boy's fate if Eric hadn't rescued him all those years before.

Toby So Toby decides to help Leo – if only for today.

Young Man 7 And maybe, after Leo cleans himself up –

Toby Toby might decide to fuck him again.

Young Man 3 In the weeks that followed, Leo returned to Toby's apartment with increasing frequency. The pattern was always the same. Toby would text Leo:

Toby Need to do some laundry?

Leo Yes.

Young Man 5 They would have sex while Leo's clothes dried.

Toby And Toby always made Leo cum.

Young Man 7 And he always paid Leo double his rate.

Leo Toby, you gave me too much.

Toby Keep it. Walking-around money.

Leo You keep fucking me like that and I'm not going to be able to walk at all.

Toby Yeah, we're good at that, you and me.

Leo I'll get out of your hair now.

Toby You wanna stay for dinner?

Leo You don't / have to –

Toby I was going to order some takeout. You hungry?

Leo I could eat.

Toby Great. Stay for dinner.

Leo You don't have to –

Toby Chinese okay? Or maybe Mexican?

Leo I like Mexican.

Toby Let's do Thai.

He takes out his phone and places an order.

Leo What do you do? For work, I mean?

Toby I'm a writer.

Leo Oh. Cool. What kind?

Toby The unappreciated kind.

Leo I don't understand.

Toby Nothing. I wrote a novel that I turned into a play that's going to Broadway in the fall.

Leo Oh. Cool.

Toby Do you go to the theatre?

Leo No.

Toby That was a stupid question.

Leo Why / is it stupid?

Toby Never mind.

Leo I'd like to.

Toby Yeah?

  Leo nods.

What are you doing Friday? I've got tickets to *Julius Caesar*. Do you want to come see some Shakespeare in the Park with me?

Leo I don't know Shakespeare.

Toby Well, he's dead, so you can't.

Leo I mean . . . I don't know his plays.

Toby We'll start with *Julius Caesar*. It'll be a fun night out.

Leo Why don't you have any books?

Toby (*looking around*) I used to. I lost them all in the move.

Leo Like, the movers lost your books?

Toby No, my ex. He took them.

Leo Oh. Are you gonna get more?

Toby I should, shouldn't I?

Leo You're a writer.

Toby I am, aren't I?
  Where are you staying these days, Leo?

Leo Around.

Toby You wanna narrow that down a bit?

Leo I crash with friends sometimes.

Toby And other times?

  Leo doesn't answer.

You know you can always crash with me if you ever
needed to.

Leo I don't like staying with clients.

Toby I'm not a client, I'm Toby! It's not like I'm asking
you to marry me, for Christ's sake.

Leo That would definitely cost extra.

Toby And if you have a policy against staying with clients,
I could always fuck you for free.

Leo Or we could just not fuck.

Toby Where's the fun in that? Besides, you like it when
I fuck you.

Leo Oh yeah? Says who?

Toby Says that cum cannon of yours. In fact, I wanna
make you cum again right now.

Leo You think you can?

Toby You're nineteen and I'm great in bed. Yes, I can
definitely make you cum again.

Leo Okay.

Toby Toby made Leo come again.

Young Man 2 Leo then stayed for dinner.

Young Man 5 And a movie.

Young Man 6 Toby showed him *The Deer Hunter.*

Young Man 3 And then, before he left –

Toby Toby made Leo come a third time.

Young Man 8 Later that week, Toby took Leo to Central Park for the Public Theater's controversial staging of *Julius Caesar.*

Young Man 7 Leo didn't understand what was being said in the play –

Young Man 3 – but he was moved nonetheless by the emotions.

Young Man 7 And then one Sunday afternoon in July –

Toby Toby took Leo to the Strand Bookstore to rebuild his collection from scratch.

2. *Strand Bookstore*

Toby Okay, I want to grab everything Doris Kearns Goodwin ever wrote. Also Barbara Tuchman. And David McCullough, too. Any book on Lincoln, I want. Any book on Gandhi, too. I want books on slavery but not the Civil War.

Young Man 8 World War Two?

Toby No.

Young Man 5 Holocaust?

Toby Yes. Nothing about Israel and Palestine. (Fucks with the feng shui.)

Young Man 3 Crusades?

Toby No.

Young Man 6 Bubonic plague?

Toby Yes.

Young Man 4 Rwanda?

Toby Yes.

Young Man 7 Apartheid?

Toby No. I want books on science but only the kind that are written as literature. Get me books on Hitler, Einstein, Mary Magdalene, Oliver Cromwell, John Muir, the space program –

Young Man 7 I've got Hitler!

Toby Neanderthals, Buddhism, organic farming –

Young Man 6 I've got Oliver Cromwell!

Toby String Theory, the Kennedy Assassination –

Young Man 8 I've got Neanderthals!

Toby Early Hollywood history –

Young Man 5 I've got String Theory!

Toby – and Chita Rivera. (*Then:*) We should get some books for you while we're at it.

Leo You don't have to get me / anything.

Toby Stop it. You're a reader. You should have books.

Young Man 7 Leo was dazzled by Toby's virtuosic display of intellect.

Young Man 2 What a mind Toby had!

Young Man 8 If only Leo could talk like that, think like that.

Young Man 3 How much better would his life be!

Young Man 2 I've got Chita!

Toby Okay, let's make this easy on ourselves. We'll pick a country and start there.

Leo plucks a volume from the shelf.

Young Man 6 Jane Austen.

Toby Okay, the Brits. So: *Pride and Prejudice*, *Sense and Sensibility*, *Emma* and *Persuasion*.

Leo We're getting *all* of these?

Toby Yes!

Young Man 7 Toby had never read any Jane Austen novels.

Young Man 6 But in most cases he had seen the movies.

Toby Okay, the Brontës! Let's get *Jane Eyre* for Charlotte, *Wuthering Heights* for Emily.

Young Man 8 What about Anne?

Toby Fuck Anne.

Young Man 4 Chaucer?

Toby Snoozefest.

Young Man 4 Conrad?

Toby Grab *Heart of Darkness*. Okay, Dickens –

Leo Toby, there's your book!

Toby Oh yeah.

Leo There's a lot of copies.

Toby Yeah, what the fuck?

Leo takes one, flips through it.

Leo What's it about?

Toby Me. My life. Well, a slice of it.

Young Man 8 Leo imagined what it might be like to be as knowledgable, as well-educated as Toby.

Leo Should I get it?

Toby hesitates, then puts it back on the shelf.

Toby Brits first, then Americans.
Great Expectations, *David Copperfield*, *Oliver Twist*. Jesus, did he only ever write about orphans?

Young Man 6 But how could Leo possibly catch up with Toby, who had been reading since childhood?

Toby What's next?

Young Man 2 *Middlemarch*?

Toby You'll never finish it but you should at least start it.

Young Man 4 And then Leo plucked a book off the shelf . . .

Toby What'd you get?

Leo E. M. Forster?

Toby Which one?

Leo (*pronouncing it 'Maur-eese'*) *Maurice*?

Toby It's pronounced 'Mor-ice'.

Young Man 7 Hugh Grant, James Wilby.

Toby It's a gay novel Forster wrote back in the teens.

Leo He wrote this when he was a teenager?

Toby No, numbskull. In 'the teens'. Like now, but a hundred years ago. That's actually one of Eric's favorite books.

Leo Who's Eric?

Toby Grab it. Also *Room with a View*.

Young Man 7 Maggie Smith, Helena Bonham Carter.

Toby Oh and *Howards End*.

Young Man 7 Emma Thompson, Vanessa Redgrave.

Leo's phone dings.

Leo Oh . . . I have to go.

Toby What, right now?

Leo Yeah, um. I, um, I just have to be somewhere.

Toby But we're only up to the 'F's.'

Leo Yeah, I know, I just . . . I gotta go.

Toby Go where? I thought we were hanging out today.

Leo I know, these plans just came up.

Toby But *we* have plans.

Leo I know, but these are . . . 'plans'.

Toby Oh. So say no. I thought we could go to the movies / or something.

Leo I can't . . . he's a regular.

Toby How many regulars do you have, exactly?

Leo A few.

Toby I didn't realize you were so popular.

Leo You're the only one I hang out with in bookstores.

Toby Do you still want your books?

Leo Yes. Very much. If you still want to get them for me. Or just one would be fine.

Toby Can I see you later?

Leo I'll text you. I'm sorry. When he calls, I have to – I have to go.

Toby stands there alone with all of Leo's books.

3. Rehearsal

Young Man 2 Adam McDowell was just weeks away from making one of the most thrilling Broadway debuts in recent memory.

Young Man 8 Adam McDowell was going to be a star.

Young Man 7 Adam McDowell was going to win the Tony.

Adam Adam McDowell had never been more frightened in all his life.

Young Man 2 Rehearsals had been tense from day one.

Adam approaches Toby.

Adam Hey, Toby?

Toby Yes, Adam?

Adam You got a minute?

Toby Sure.

Adam I had a question about page 74.

Toby It is often to be found after page 73.

Adam I had a question about this new line you wrote. I didn't used to say it in Chicago.

Toby Yes?

Adam Right here where Elan says to Agatha: '*Et tu Brutus*,' you're obviously quoting from *Julius Caesar*, right?

Toby Correct.

Adam Okay. So. Here's the thing. It's actually '*Et tu, Brute*' not '*Brutus*'. '*Brute*' being the vocative case for '*Brutus*', which is of course a second declension masculine noun.

Toby What's your point, Adam?

Adam Well I'm wondering if you got that wrong on purpose or . . . ?

Toby Or what?

Adam It's just that you make a point of having Elan be this incredibly well-read and precocious seventeen-year-old. Like, kind of a genius.

Toby Yes, Adam. That hasn't changed.

Adam I don't know if that's true. Because if he's getting basic Latin wrong, that in fact changes everything.

Toby How so?

Adam Well it means he's full of shit, right? It makes him kind of a fraud. It's confusing to me because it's inconsistent with what we know about the character.

Toby And so . . . ?

Adam And so I was hoping we could just . . . get the line right.

A beat, then:

Toby 'Get it right'?

Adam Yeah, Toby. You should probably get the famous quote right.

Toby I'd like to hear the line as I have written it.

Adam But what you've written makes no sense.

Toby It makes sense to me.

Adam Then *you* play the fucking scene! All I am asking for is just a little bit of help from you. I am up on that stage for an hour and forty-seven minutes without a single break. And I have to imagine that if I were any other actor in this company or any other actor in the world, you wouldn't think twice about granting my simple and very respectful request. But because it's me, because you've decided you hate me / after telling me that you love me –

Toby Keep your voice down, Adam. Keep your fucking voice down / Adam. I never told you I –

Adam Oh I'm sorry, am I embarrassing you?

Toby I never said that I loved you.

By now the Lads (playing actors in Toby's play) start to pay attention to this exchange.

Adam You attacked me and groped me / and declared your love for me.

Toby I never groped you! I never groped him.

Adam That night in my apartment in Chicago?

Toby You were telling me a story about getting gang-fucked by twenty Bel Ami models!

Adam Shut the fuck up, Toby!

Toby Oh, *now* you feel like whispering!

Adam Please, Toby. Don't push me away. I need your friendship. I need you / on my side.

Toby (*exploding*) I'm not your fucking mentor, Adam, and I'm not your fucking friend!

He hurls the script down at Adam's feet. Dead silence in the rehearsal room. All eyes on Toby.

Adam wants to make a change on page 74. Let's give the princess what she wants.

Toby storms out of the room.

4. Bar

Eric Hey.

Toby Hey. You look good.

Eric Thanks. Thanks for seeing me.

Toby Yeah.

Eric Is this weird?

Toby I thought it would be, but it's actually nice to see you again.

Eric Well, good.
How are rehearsals going?

Toby Great. Tom's a genius, blah blah.

Eric And . . . and Adam?

Toby Adam's fine.

Eric Tell him, tell him I said hello.

Toby You know, you really do look great.

Eric Did you not mean it when you said it just a minute ago?

Toby I just realized how much I meant it.

Eric Well, thank you.

Toby Did you change your hair?

Eric No.

Toby Looks different.

Eric It isn't.

Toby Huh.

Eric I still have your boxes, by the way.

Toby My – ?

Eric Your parents' things.

Toby That's what you wanted to see me about?

Eric No, I –

Toby You didn't have to keep them.

Eric I just figured you might want them someday.

Toby You do look really great, Eric.

Eric I believe you. Listen, Toby, the reason I asked you here today / is that I –

Toby I'm glad you did because I just realized that there's something I need to say to you.

Eric I'm sure there's a lot we have to say to each other.

Toby Yeah, but it's something I just realized.

Eric Great. But if I could maybe go first –

Toby I made a mistake letting you go.

Silence, then . . .

Eric Oh Toby.

Toby Wow. It's been a long time since I heard you say that.

Eric Toby, listen, I –

Toby I know, I know. We haven't seen each other in months. And the break-up was ugly. But I can't seem to move on from you.

Eric Toby.

Toby I just . . . I didn't realize just how much you kept me together. And now seeing you again, being with you, it just feels so right. Like I'm . . . like I'm coming home.

Eric Toby –

Toby Oh fuck, Eric, I made such a terrible mistake and I want you back.

Eric Toby you don't / understand.

Toby I love you, Eric. And I'm completely lost without you.

Eric Toby, I'm getting married.

The Grand Canyon.

Toby What?

Eric I'm getting married. In October.

Toby To who?

Eric Henry Wilcox.

Silence. Then Toby starts laughing.

Toby That's – You're good – I – Wow you really – I totally fell for that.

Eric I'm not joking.

Toby Okay, Eric. You got me once.

Eric Toby, I'm marrying Henry Wilcox.

Toby No, you're not.

Eric Yes, I am.

Toby Stop that.

Eric I'm marrying Henry.

Toby Why do you keep saying that?

Eric Because it's true.

Toby Fuck you.

Eric Excuse me?

Toby I just poured my heart out to you and you go and do this to me? Fuck you, Eric.

Eric This isn't about you, Toby.

Toby Yes, it is! We're together for seven years and then seven *months* go by and now you love him and you're marrying this guy?

Eric You left me, remember? For Adam. My life is none of your business anymore.

Toby Please, Eric. I need you. I'm falling apart without you.

Eric I have spent the last seven months in more pain than I have ever been in because of you. And I finally find just a fraction of the happiness I felt with you and you do this to me. It is so unfair of you.

Toby You're making the worst mistake of your life.

Eric No, Toby. *You're* the worst mistake of my life.

Toby But I love you, Eric.

Eric I pray that one day you'll be able to say that to someone and actually mean it.

5. Toby's Agent

Young Man 5 Toby gets a call from his agent.

Agent What the hell happened today?

Toby What do you mean?

Agent Tom wants you out of the room.

Toby What do you mean, 'out of the room'?

Agent As in barred from rehearsals.

Toby They can't fire me from my own play.

Agent Adam doesn't feel safe with you in the room.

Toby He said that?!

Agent He's filing a complaint with Equity.

Toby That duplicitous little twink and his pederastic Svengali. I'll pull the rights.

Agent And you will never get produced in New York again.

Toby Why aren't you fighting for me?

Agent I am, but you are making it really difficult. You threw your script at Adam?

Toby Not at his head! How long am I barred from rehearsals?

Agent I'm sure it will blow over in a few days . . . definitely by tech . . . I'll see if I can get you into previews.

Toby 'Get me in'? It's my play!

Agent Well, unless you have four million dollars with which to produce it yourself when your producers walk away from it, that's not going to do you much good.

Toby This is fucking bullshit! I'll sue them!

Agent No, you will not. You're going to take a vacation.

Toby I don't want to take a vacation, I want to work on my play.

Agent You said so yourself: the play is done. Let them finish rehearsals. Go to the beach. Take one of the twenty-nothings you're fucking these days and leave Tom and Adam to their work.

Toby Toby hangs up on his agent, blistering with rage. He calls Adam and immediately gets his voicemail.

Adam Beep.

Toby You would be nothing without me, do you understand? You would be nothing without this part. I gave you this chance, *I'm* the one who made it happen. ME! It wasn't Tom and his magical fifty-year-old Viagra dick, which by now I'm sure has given you herpes. I will never speak to you again, I don't ever even want to look at you again. And when you win the Tony for this role – WHICH YOU HAD FUCKING BETTER – it will be because of me and the part that I've written. So if you don't thank me in your acceptance speech – and I mean, like really lick my ass – I will make sure that everyone knows how you *betrayed* me and what a back-stabbing, malicious, cock-teasing little Eve Harrington you are. And just for the record: Ben Platt, Lucas Hedges, and Timothé Chalamet all passed on this part before we offered it to you. So you should probably thank them in your Tony speech, too. So in conclusion: *fuck you, Adam!* I wish I'd never –

Adam BEEP!

Toby Toby storms into his apartment, grabs his computer and his credit card and, without hesitation, rents a cottage on Fire Island through the end of the summer.

Young Man 7 The cost is astronomical.

Toby Toby doesn't care about the fucking cost.

Young Man 5 All Toby can think about is his desperate need to escape the city.

Young Man 8 Escape Adam.

Young Man 6 Escape Eric.

Young Man 7 Escape his play.

Young Man 4 Escape himself.

Young Man 3 Toby then texts Leo:

Toby Do you want to come with me to Fire Island for the next six weeks?

Young Man 3 And Toby almost instantly gets an answer:

Leo Yes.

End of Scene Three.

SCENE FOUR

Summer 2017

1. Fire Island

The sound of the ocean.

Leo Leo had never seen the ocean.

Young Man 4 Never walked on a beach or felt the pull of undertow on his feet.

Young Man 6 His fears –

Young Man 5 – his misfortunes –

Young Man 6 – his entire life history momentarily vanished in the face of such immensity.

Young Man 4 For the first time in his life, Leo felt he had sufficient room to breathe.

Young Man 2 He packed an old roll-behind suitcase that rattled along the boardwalk, filled with all the books Toby had bought him.

Young Man 3 He would wake early each morning and walk along the beach as the sun was rising –

Young Man 4 – eventually planting himself in the sand to read.

Young Man 8 Leo tore through his books at an almost frantic pace.

Young Man 1 Jane Austen.

Young Man 2 Charles Dickens.

Young Man 3 Christopher Isherwood.

Young Man 4 Zadie Smith.

Young Man 5 Charlotte Brontë.

Young Man 6 Hilary Mantel.

Young Man 7 David Mitchell.

Young Man 8 Evelyn Waugh.

Young Man 6 Leo read like an addict, his mind expanding with every novel.

Young Man 2 Emily Brontë.

Young Man 3 Alan Hollinghurst.

Young Man 4 Lawrence Durrell.

Young Man 5 Graham Greene.

Young Man 7 Virginia Woolf.

Young Man 6 E. M. Forster.

Young Man 4 Leo opened *Howards End* and from the first sentence, his life forever changed.

Leo 'One may as well begin with Helen's letters to her sister.'

Young Man 8 What was it about Forster that spoke to him out of all the other writers he encountered that summer?

Leo While the world Forster wrote about no longer existed, his characters hummed with a human truth – he felt their vibrations.

Young Man 8 It was when he opened *Maurice* that Leo understood the reason for his bond with Forster.

Leo Like the character of Maurice Hall, Leo had spent his life feeling lonely and unloved –

Young Man 3 – damaged beyond redemption.

Young Man 2 Leo understood the simple yet powerful connection of a gay man in the early twentieth century speaking directly to a young gay man at the start of the twenty-first.

Leo Forster was the first writer to reach a hand out to Leo and say –

Young Man 4 'I have felt as you feel. You are not alone. I will be with you always.'

Toby Jesus! We're on motherfucking Fire Island! The last thing anyone comes here to do is *read*! Let's dance, let's drink, let's get fucked up!

Leo By they end of their first week, Toby and Leo had become regular fixtures at dances, at house parties. Their faces were familiar to people they passed every day on the boardwalk and on the beach.

Toby Have you ever done coke?

Leo I've only ever smoked pot.

Toby Today you're getting an upgrade. (*To Young Man 5.*) Gimme an 8-Ball. Plus a teen. What else you got?

Young Man 5 Molly.

Toby Yeah. Six pills. No, make it ten.

Young Man 5 Want any K?

Toby Nah, but gimme some G. Six caps. What else you got? I want something I haven't tried.

Young Man 5 Have you ever tried crystal?

Toby I'm not that kind of gay.

Young Man 5 Tina makes sex amazing. You will fuck like you have never fucked before, I promise.

Toby looks at Leo.

Toby You wanna try it?

Leo I'll do it if you do it.

Toby We'll probably hate it and never do it again.

Leo Leo discovered that he loved it.

Young Man 8 And of course there was sex.

Young Man 7 Sex was everywhere.

Young Man 4 In the heat of the sun –

Young Man 3 – and the shade of the dunes.

Young Man 6 In the music and the dancing–

Young Man 5 – in the pools and hot tubs –

Young Man 3 – and along the twisty pathways of the Meat Rack.

Young Man 2 Fueled by the crystal, Toby and Leo danced and partied and fucked each other constantly.

Leo Neither of them had ever had sex like the kind they had on crystal.

Young Man 7 Toby devoured Leo's body.

Young Man 8 As if Toby was addicted to him.

Leo Over time, Leo learned to give himself over so openly, so unapologetically to Toby's desire. It was different from the kind of sex he was accustomed to. It approached what Leo suspected might be called lovemaking.

2. *Party in The Pines*

A great dance party.

Young Man 5 How are you boys feeling?

Leo Soooo gooood.

Toby This Molly you gave us is like silk.

Young Man 5 Are you and your boyfriend staying in the Pines?

Leo Oh, we're not –

Toby Yes, we are.

Young Man 5 We should hang out. You two are such a hot couple.

Toby Who? Me and Leo?

Young Man 5 You've been turning heads since you got here.

Toby You hear that, Leo? We've been turning heads.

Young Man 5 My roommates are throwing a party tonight. You should come with me.

Toby We like parties, don't we, Leo?

    Leo nods.

Young Man 5 You like this kind of party?

Young Man 5 holds up his phone and plays a video of an orgy.

Toby Oh shit.

Young Man 5 Yeah. There's a full-on fuckfest happening at my place right now. My friends have been wanting a piece of your boyfriend's hot little ass since you got here. Are you into sharing your toys? (*Then, holding up a packet of crystal.*) I'm definitely into sharing mine. Come to the party and you can have all you want.

Toby and Leo look at each other as if to confer. It's clear Leo doesn't want to go.

Toby Have you ever done anything like that before?

Leo No.

Toby Neither have I.

Young Man 5 Come and join us, boys.

Toby Let's do it.

Leo I don't really wanna –

Toby Oh no, come on!

Leo Why don't you go without me?

Toby No! I wanna watch all those guys with their hands all over you. Sucking you. Fucking you. It's why we came here, isn't it?

Leo I came here to be with you.

Toby No arguments – we're going.

Young Man 5 And so Leo went to the party. Where Toby watched him get fucked by his dealer and his friends.

Toby (*to Young Man 5*) What else you got?

Young Man 6 More guys show up, each wanting to have a turn with Leo.

Young Man 2 Some grabbing at him so hard that bruises start to form on Leo's wrists.

Leo Toby?

Young Man 7 Toby watches them sucking Leo off –

Young Man 3 – rubbing his body –

Young Man 2 – eating him out –

Young Man 4 – kissing him all over.

Young Man 7 Someone grabs Leo's hair.

Young Man 8 Another holds Leo down.

Young Man 7 As one by one they take their turn with him.

Leo Toby –

Toby God, baby you look so hot.

Young Man 6 Everyone is touching Leo.

Young Man 5 Thirty hands, fifteen mouths on his body.

Leo Toby?

Toby And Toby thinks to himself, I always want to feel like I do right now. This moment, this feeling. I want to live in this moment for the rest of my life.

3. *A Cottage in Cherry Grove*

Leo They get back to their cottage and Leo takes the hottest shower he can stand. He cleans himself and discovers he is bleeding. He can see it going down the drain.

He cleans up as best he can and crawls into bed, grateful that the night is over and he can wake in the morning and return to his books. But when it happens the next weekend, when it happens every weekend . . .

4. *Toby and Leo's Bedroom*

Toby enters. Leo is in bed, reading.

Toby Hey, there you are. Come on – a bunch of us are going over to Richie and Joe's for a swim.

Leo I don't really feel like walking all the way to the Pines tonight. Why don't we just stay in?

Toby No, it'll be fun. Richie just brought some coke back from the city.

Leo But I'm reading.

Toby What are you reading now? (*Peeking at the cover.*) *Maurice*? But you've read that already.

Leo I know, but I –

Toby Come on, let's go.

Leo Why did you become a writer?

Toby I dunno. I have an overactive imagination and I detest manual labor. Come on, get changed.

Leo Did you start writing, like, as a kid, or –

Toby Who are you? Barbara Walters all of a sudden? What's with all the questions? Chop, chop.

Leo I was just curious. You gave me all these books to read but you never talk about your own writing. You never talk about your life.

Toby You never talk about *your* life. Come on, let's go.

Leo What do you want to know?

Toby Where are you from, Leo?

Leo Oklahoma, where are you from?

Toby Where are your parents?

Leo I don't know, where are yours?

Toby When did you come to New York?

Leo Two years ago. Who's Adam?

Beat.

Toby Why are you asking me about my writing? What? Are you thinking of becoming a writer, too?

Leo No, of course not.

Toby Why 'of course'?

Leo Well, I didn't go to college or anything.

Toby So?

Leo I didn't even . . . I didn't finish high school.

Toby Neither did I.

Leo No. You had to have gone to college.

Toby I dropped out of high school my junior year. I moved to New York and started writing.

Leo I thought you were a trust fund kid who went to fancy schools and had everything handed to you without working for it.

Toby Yeah, I know you did. The truth is I've worked hard for every dollar I've ever made.

Leo So have I.

Toby Yeah. Well . . .

Leo What am I to you, Toby?

Toby What do you / mean?

Leo When we're alone together you can be sweet and kind and loving. And then when we leave this house, all you want to do is share me with your friends like a joint.

Toby Leo –

Leo How can I mean so much to you and so little?

Toby Whoa, wait a minute.

Leo Am I a part of your life at all or am I just here for you and your friends to fuck?

Toby Wait, I thought you liked that.

Leo No, Toby, I hate it. You like it, which is why I do it.

Toby You can always say no.

Leo (*not buying it*) Can I?

Toby Why would you think you can't?

Leo Because you're paying for everything, including me.

Toby Leo, I invited you here as my guest.

Leo So why are you treating me like your whore?

Toby Leo –

Leo I don't know if I'm supposed to be falling in love with you / or if I should just send you a bill for my time –

Toby Whoa, whoa, whoa . . . Who said anything about falling in love?

This takes the wind out of Leo.

Leo Oh God, I'm so stupid. Do I mean anything to you at all?

Toby Leo – yes, of course.

Leo What, then? What do I mean to you? What do you want from me?

Silence. Then:

Toby I want you because your eyes / are the most –

Leo Please don't answer me like a writer. Answer me like a real person. Who are you, Toby?

5. *Eric's Voicemails*

Eric Toby, hey. It's me.
I hate to leave this on your voicemail, but we need to find some kind of peace with each other if we're ever going to fully heal. Call me when you're ready.

Toby Delete.

Eric Hey, Toby, it's me. I hope the reason you haven't called back is because you're busy with previews. I hope things are going well.

Toby Delete.

Eric All right, so clearly you're not going to call me back. Henry and I are getting married in two weeks – we're actually calling it a celebration of marriage. Anyway, despite all that's gone on between us this past year, I'd like you to be there. I'm sending an invitation. It's the Saturday after your opening. Call me back.

Toby Delete.

Eric Toby, hi. I know your play is opening tonight. I know how hard you worked for this. You should be proud. My wedding's on Saturday. I would love to have you there. Break a leg tonight.

After a moment:

Toby Delete.

6. *Toby's Opening*

Toby Toby's play opens, as all important plays do, on a Thursday.

Young Man 5 Toby buys Leo a custom-made suit for the occasion.

Young Man 6 Leo has never owned a suit before.

Young Man 2 Or anything as nice as this.

Young Man 7 He protests when he hears the sales clerk quoting Toby its price.

Young Man 8 Leo could rent a small apartment for what this suit costs.

Young Man 3 But housing is no longer a concern for Leo.

Young Man 4 He's been staying with Toby since they returned from Fire Island.

Young Man 8 Toby buys Leo clothes.

Young Man 3 And even more books.

Young Man 4 And now this suit.

Young Man 5 Leo has no idea how to put it on.

Young Man 7 The pants he can do.

Young Man 2 And the shirt.

Young Man 6 But then he realizes the sleeves have no buttons.

Young Man 5 Leo has no idea what to do with the cuff links.

Young Man 7 Nor does he know how to tie a tie.

Young Man 2 He has to look it up on YouTube.

Young Man 5 Leo attempts it twenty-seven times until he gets it right.

Young Man 3 But when he puts on the jacket –

Young Man 4 – splashes himself with a little of the Santal 33 Toby has bought him for the occasion –

Young Man 8 – and Leo looks at himself in the mirror –

Leo – standing in Toby's apartment, wearing a new designer suit, Leo takes a breath and pretends for one, two, three seconds, that he belongs here, in this apartment, in this man's life. For the briefest moment, Leo allows himself to believe that he is home.

Toby They arrive at the theatre.

Young Man 5 Toby charges toward the step-and-repeat, basking in the glow of his moment of triumph.

Toby As he stands there being photographed, Toby looks out at the sea of people crowding around the theatre and he realizes that he knows no one. His agents are here. And the producers. There are some famous people. But where are his friends? Where are his people? Where's Eric?

Young Man 2 Toby, look over here.

Young Man 7 Don't forget to smile.

Toby Toby glances up at the marquee, catching sight of his name: 'LOVED BOY – A PLAY BY TOBY DARLING'. And for a second, his eyes register it as 'Loved Boy, a Lie by Toby Darling'.

Young Man 3 Toby, over here!

Young Man 4 Toby, big smile.

Toby And in that moment, Toby knows that Eric was right.

Young Man 5 Toby, who designed your suit?

Young Man 8 Toby, what a night for you!

Toby That his book was a lie and his play was even more of one.

Young Man 6 Toby, how do you feel?

Toby And soon all of New York is going to see it and no one will know who Toby Darling really is.

Young Man 3 Toby looks up and sees Leo.

Young Man 7 Their eyes meet.

Young Man 6 Leo stares at him with a look that can only be described as love.

Young Man 4 And Toby thinks to himself –

Toby He is all that I have in this world.

Young Man 8 Toby leans over and whispers into Leo's ear:

Toby I'm so happy that you're here.

Young Man 5 They take their seats.

Young Man 4 The house lights dim –

Young Man 5 – and the lights slowly rise on Adam McDowell.

Leo Leo gasps at the sight of him. There before him, Leo sees himself. But not himself. Leo cannot help but see his face in Adam's. The same eyes – except Adam's are more hopeful. The same lips – except Adam's form more naturally into a smile. Adam McDowell is what Leo might look like if he had ever been loved. Leo turns to Toby, seeking confirmation that he is not crazy for seeing the resemblance. But Toby is too focused on Adam to notice. And the look on Toby's face tells Leo a simple and heartbreaking story: Toby is desperately in love with Adam McDowell. Leo watches Toby watching Adam and in that moment, Leo understands he is nothing more than a substitute, a poor copy of a remarkable original. Leo wants to cry, Leo wants to scream, Leo wants to run out of the theatre and not stop until the river swallows him.

But he is forced to stay there as the play unfolds, watching Adam: his twin, his negation. By the time the play ends, Leo is obliterated.

Toby Hey! What's the matter?

Leo I have to go.

Young Man 2 Congratulations, Toby!

Toby What's going on?

Young Man 3 Toby, that was beautiful!

Leo I can't do this.

Toby What do you mean?

Leo I can't be here. With you.

Toby Wait, hold on –!

Young Man 4 Hey Toby, congratulations. Do you have a minute to –

Toby (*to Young Man 4*) Just gimme a second. (*To Leo.*) Leo, what's the matter?

Leo I'm not who you want, Toby.

Young Man 3 Toby, I told you that you were going to be a big deal someday.

Toby What are you talking about?

Leo You called me Adam the night we met. And the morning I came back.

Young Man 7 Toby, some of the investors want to get their pictures with you and Adam.

Toby Leo, no.

Leo You're in love with Adam, not me.

Toby No, Leo, that isn't true.

Leo You actually made me believe that you wanted me.

Young Man 8 Is that Adam McDowell?

Young Man 4 Jesus, that kid looks just like Adam McDowell.

Young Man 3 Maybe he's Adam McDowell's understudy?

Young Man 5 Toby, can we get that picture now?

Leo I'm just a whore you picked up because I look like someone else. You made me believe I was special, that I belong here. But I don't belong here.

Toby Yes, you do, because I want you to be here. Leo, wait!
  I want you in my life. I want you because you remind me of myself when I was your age. I want you because I know what it's like to want something more than what you've been given. I want you because you once asked me to rescue you without knowing that the night we met, I desperately needed rescuing, too. I love you, Leo. And I'm so sorry I didn't realize that until tonight.

Leo Leo's head says run, but his heart say stay. And for the first time in his life, Leo decides to trust.

Young Man 3 An hour later, the reviews start to pour in. Toby's play is a smash.

End of Scene Four.

SCENE FIVE

Autumn 2017

1. Henry's Estate in Dutchess County

Young Man 6 The morning of Eric and Henry's wedding dawned crisp, clear and bright. A perfect autumn day.

Eric Glass woke with a sense of optimism he had not known in quite some time.

Eric in a new suit. Henry enters.

Henry Last chance to flee.

Eric In these shoes, are you joking?

Henry You do look very handsome.

Eric Do I? I've never owned a suit as nice as this. It's certainly a step up from my bar mitzvah suit. In fact, I think this suit might've cost more than my bar mitzvah.

Henry But, God knows, not as much as your wedding.

Eric Our wedding.

Henry Yes.

Eric This will be a fun day, I promise.

Henry I believe that's true.

Henry is overcome with emotions, pulls Eric tightly to him in a deep, tender embrace.

There will be days when you do not feel as tightly held by me as you are right now. But never doubt my gratitude. You've reminded me what it's like to be hopeful, to respond to life with excitement and wonder. You are joy personified, Eric Glass. And I am so grateful you have chosen to spend your life with me.

Young Man 6 And with that, Eric Glass and Henry Wilcox went outside to greet their guests on the lawn of Henry's Dutchess County estate. They exchanged brief vows. There was music and dancing, there was champagne and a dozen different cakes. The sun sparkled through the autumn leaves. Neither Eric nor Henry could remember a more perfect day.

Young Man 2 And then –

Young Man 3 – a taxi drove up the gravel driveway toward the house.

Young Man 2 A few heads turned in its direction.

Young Man 3 Most did not notice.

Eric But Eric did.

Young Man 4 For out of that taxi climbed Toby Darling. And with him was . . .

Eric Adam?

Young Man 5 As they drew closer, Eric could see that it was not in fact Adam McDowell but rather a young man who bore an astonishing resemblance to him.

Young Man 8 Neither he nor Toby looked like they'd slept in days.

Toby enters with Leo in tow.

Toby Eric! Eric Glass!

Eric Toby?

Toby Eric! Get in the car. We can all escape together.

Eric Toby, what are you doing?

Toby Rescuing you!

Eric You are coked out of your mind.

Toby Come on, we've got to get you out of here.

Eric Toby, please don't do this.

Leo Toby, maybe this was a bad idea.

Eric Yes, Toby, listen to your friend.

Toby His name is Leo. He's my boyfriend. We're in love.

Eric I don't give a shit! I want you both to leave right now.

Toby You invited us!

Eric Not to do this!

Toby You don't need to marry Henry. You don't need his house, his money. Let me show you that I can be a better person. Look: I *can* love! See? I'm in love with Leo but you're not in love with Henry.

The Jasons approach.

Jason 1 Is everything okay?

Jason 2 Toby, you made it!

Toby Oh good! Reinforcements! Jason, tell Eric he's making a terrible mistake.

Leo Toby, maybe this isn't such a good idea.

Jason 1 Toby, what do you think you're doing?

Toby I'm saving Eric!

Leo Maybe we should go.

Tristan enters.

Tristan Toby you have *got* to go.

Leo Toby, maybe we / should go.

Tristan Toby, get the fuck outta here.

Jason 1 Come on, Toby, why don't you and I take a walk?

Toby Oh, fuck off, Jason.

Jason 1 Toby, I'm serious, man.

Toby Get your hands off me, Jason.

Leo Toby, please, let's just go.

Jason 1 I'm not going to ask you again, Toby.

Toby Oh fuck you, Jason.

Eric, I will make up to you everything that I've done wrong.

Eric Including right now? Only you could crash a wedding you were actually invited to.

Toby It isn't a wedding, it's a *celebration of marriage*!

On that last line, Toby grandly swings his arms out and accidentally hits Eric in the face.

Eric Toby, Jesus!

Jason 1 That's it, Toby.

Jason 1 socks Toby in the face. Toby falls backwards on his ass.

Toby ⎫ Fuck you, Jason! I think you broke my nose. I'll sue you!

Jason 1 ⎭ Ow! I've never punched someone before. That fucking hurts!

Jason 2 ⎰ Baby, holy shit! You just punched Toby in the face!

Leo ⎱ Toby, Toby, let's go. We shouldn't be here.

Eric ⎰ Toby, leave, and take your boyfriend with you.

Tristan ⎱ Your nose isn't broken, Toby. Now hit the fuckin' road.

Henry storms on.

Henry What the hell is going on? Toby?

Eric They were just leaving, Henry.

Toby No, we were not. We were invited!

Henry Toby, get the hell off my property.

Toby I won't let you ruin his life. Eric deserves to be happy.

228

Eric I *am* happy!

Henry I'm calling the police.

Eric No, let's just get them back into their taxi and . . .

Leo Henry!

Silence. All eyes on Leo. Henry is frozen. He and Leo stare at each other in disbelief.

Henry What are you doing here?

Leo I'm sorry, Henry. I didn't know.

Henry What is he doing here?

Eric Toby brought him. Do you know him?

Henry (*to Toby*) You sick piece of shit. What the fuck do you think you're trying to prove?

Toby Me? Fuck you, asshole. How do you know my boyfriend?

Eric Henry . . . ?

Henry Get them out of here.

Eric Henry . . .

Henry *Now!*

He storms off. Eric looks at Toby.

Eric Leave.

Toby Eric –

Eric LEAVE ME ALONE!

Leo Toby, let's go.

Toby Eric, I'm sorry –

Eric I once loved you, Toby, but I am cured of that. Everything you touch you destroy. You are unhappy and unloved because you deserve to be. I now understand why your father killed himself, why your mother drank herself to death. They did it to get as far away from you as possible. They didn't abandon you, Toby, they fled from you like the disease that you are. You will spend your life alone and, like your parents, you will die alone. I just hope for that boy's sake it happens sooner rather than later.

He runs off. The Lads follow. Toby and Leo are alone.

Leo Toby?

Toby Toby wants to reach for Eric. To rewind the last three minutes. He'd do it differently. He'd do it all differently.

Leo Toby, let's go.

Toby He would rewind to that morning, to the day he left Eric, to the moment he first reached out to Adam with desire, to the day his father died.

Leo Toby, please.

Toby He would rewind until the tape snapped free of its moorings and the story of Toby vanished from existence.

Leo Toby, I don't want to be here.

Toby But he doesn't reach for Eric and he cannot rewind his story. Toby can only go forward.

Leo Toby?

Toby But he doesn't know how.

End of Act One.

Act Two

Autumn 2017–Spring 2018

SCENE ONE
1. Henry's Estate in Dutchess County

Autumn 2017. Eric and Henry.

Henry Did you invite him?

Eric Yes.

Henry Why?

Eric I, I, I just felt –

Henry Were you trying to humiliate me?

Eric I didn't know that he was going to do that.

Henry You should have.

Eric I should have anticipated that he'd show up drunk and coked out and that he would make a scene?

Henry Yes! Because he is Toby Darling and that is what he does.

Eric Should I have also anticipated that he would bring someone you clearly have some kind of a history with?

Henry Do not turn this around on me, Eric.

Eric Who is he?

Henry He's no one, he's nothing.

Eric Didn't seem like nothing to me. How do you know him?

Henry I fucked him.

Eric When?

Henry I can't give you dates.

Eric So more than once? How did you meet him?

Henry I paid for him. He's a fucking prostitute. *You* are the one who invited him into my home.

Eric How long have you been seeing him? *Henry, answer me!*

Henry Two years, off and on.

Eric Why?

Henry Oh, don't be a child, Eric.

Eric No, I mean: why not me? Why don't you want to fuck me?

Henry I'm not having this conversation.

Eric It is the same conversation.

Henry You willfully went behind my back and invited that madman to my home.
 Are you still in love with him?

Eric Have you fucked that kid since we've been together?

Henry Yes.

Eric More than once?

Henry Yes.

Eric In our home?

Henry No. He didn't know anything about me until today.

Eric I guess that makes two of us.

Henry I have given you everything I can.

Eric Except yourself. Walter was able to tell me –

Henry *I am not Walter!* If you married me hoping to find some connection to him, you've made a terrible mistake. One that I will free you of if you want.

Eric What I want is you. All of you. You've asked me to spend my life with you and here I am, in a brand new suit, willing to give you what you've asked of me but you have given me nothing that actually costs you to give. If I can't have sex with you, then I at least deserve to know why.

Henry Because that would ask more of me than I ever want to give to anyone again. That boy lets me do what I want with him and then he goes away. He does not matter to me. You do. I don't reach out to you for the same thing because you cannot give me what he can.

Eric I've spent these months trying to accept the idea of a sexless marriage but what you're really asking me to accept is a loveless one.

Henry That is not how I see it.

Eric Did you love Walter?

Henry That is none of your business.

Young Man 4 Yes.

Eric Did you ever need him like I needed Toby?

Young Man 4 Yes, you did, Henry.

Eric WERE YOU EVER ALIVE, HENRY? HAVE YOU EVER FELT ANYTHING DEEPLY?

Young Man 3 He was so beautiful that day you first saw him. At that rooftop party, in the late afternoon sun.

Henry His hair –

Young Man 3 – was shining in the light.

Henry His skin –

Young Man 3 – was luminous and dark from his summer at the beach.

Henry His eyes –

Young Man 3 – were so –

Henry – honest.

Young Man 3 Seeing right into you. Wanting you. Drawing you to him. God, how you wanted him.
   I'm Henry.

Young Man 4 I'm Walter. You're married.

Young Man 3 No, I'm not.

Young Man 4 You've got a farmer's tan on your ring finger.

Young Man 3 God how you wanted him.

Henry He stopped my brain from working. He made the words come out all wrong.

Young Man 3 You stumbled out of the gate.
   Have you seen *E.T.* yet?

Young Man 4 Jesus, you've got kids, too?

Henry I think you're beautiful.

Young Man 3 Round and round you both went. Talking about nothing, though it felt like everything. And then finally, when you couldn't stand to wait any longer:

Henry *and* **Young Man 3** Do you want to come back to my place?

Young Man 4 Will your wife and kids be there?

Henry *and* **Young Man 3** They're away for the summer.

Henry Come back to my place.

Young Man 4 What if I don't want to leave?

Young Man 3 And in that moment, you knew you didn't want him to. And so you said:

Henry Would that be such a bad thing?

Young Man 3 Finally, you left. Your legs could not move fast enough as you ran the four blocks to your sublet.

Young Man 4 Racing up the stairs.

Young Man 3 Five fucking flights.

Young Man 4 You maneuvered so that I was in front of you.

Young Man 3 So you could stare at his ass.

Young Man 4 Finally into the apartment.

Young Man 3 Both completely naked by the time you hit the bed.

Young Man 4 God how you fucked me.

Henry God how I wanted him.

Young Man 3 God how you loved him. How it felt to swallow all the shame, the guilt, the fear.

Young Man 4 And to listen to those four words escape from your lips:

Young Man 3 As you exploded inside him:

Henry I love you, Walter.

Young Man 4 Finally, after years of fighting against it, after a lifetime of shame –

Henry – to hold you in my arms –

Young Man 3 – delighting in his body –

Henry – in your smell –

Young Man 4 – in my skin –

Henry – in your warm breath on my shoulder.

Young Man 4 I love you, Henry.

Young Man 3 And to know the peace that comes from finally telling the truth about yourself, about your heart.

Young Man 4 Then you asked me to stay.

Young Man 3 Not just that night.

Young Man 4 But for hundreds, thousands, ten thousand nights after that.

Eric When did you stop loving him, Henry? When did that end?

Young Man 3 That day at the house.

Young Man 4 You wanted to surprise me.

Henry I'd been in London, working.

Young Man 3 Hiding. Men were dying there too, but you didn't know their names.

Henry I flew home to surprise you.

Young Man 4 I ran across the yard to you.

Henry Barefoot.

Young Man 3 I almost called from the airport but I wanted to see the look on your face as I pulled up.

Young Man 4 Henry . . .

Henry God, I've missed you.

Young Man 4 Henry, Peter is here.

Henry Peter?

Young Man 3 Peter?

Eric Peter West.

Young Man 3 He's visiting?

Young Man 4 He's dying.

Henry He came here?

Young Man 4 I brought him here.

Young Man 3 To the home you bought to save him, to save yourself.

Young Man 4 He had nowhere else to go.

Henry What room is he in?

Young Man 4 Upstairs, in the room across from ours.

Young Man 3 The room where your kids sleep.

Henry Get him out of there.

Young Man 3 No, you screamed at him.

Henry YOU BROUGHT THAT DISEASE INTO OUR HOME!

Young Man 4 Henry, our friend is dying.

Young Man 3 After all these years, you can still see Walter's face in that moment, contorted with fear and confusion.

Young Man 4 *and* **Eric** Look at me.

Henry I can't.

Young Man 4 He is our responsibility.

Henry I'm responsible to you, to my boys, to myself and to no one else.

Eric You got back in the car.

Young Man 4 Henry!

Eric You drove away.

Young Man 4 You left me alone.

Eric Without so much as a phone call.

Young Man 3 And then, months later –

Young Man 4 I don't want to do this, Henry.

Young Man 3 Do you want to sell it, then?

Young Man 4 No. I want that house to be what it has always been to us.

Young Man 3 If anything were to happen to me –

Young Man 4 Nothing is going to happen to you.

Young Man 3 You could sell it, live in it, leave it to whomever you choose.

Eric Henry, if you keep running from this –

Young Man 4 – from what happened at that house, from what is happening to our friends, to our community –

Young Man 4 *and* **Eric** – you will never know peace.

Henry That is my decision.

Young Man 3 You decided that no house, no community, no nation would ever be strong enough to save you.

Eric You had to save yourself.

Young Man 3 You had to turn off the part of you that fears. The part that reaches with desire.

Eric The part that loves.

Henry I couldn't touch another man without thinking about death.

Young Man 3 And so you never touched him again. Your mouth never uttered the words 'I love you' ever again.

Henry Men were dying all around me. Men I knew. Men I loved. My friends. My peers.

Young Man 3 You decided that if you didn't love him, it wouldn't hurt as badly to lose him –

Henry For thirty-six years I held you at a distance.
  For thirty-six years I did not love you the way you needed me to.
  For thirty-six years I protected myself from the pain of losing you.

Young Man 3 And then, after thirty-six years, you lost him anyway. And it hurt just as badly as you feared it would.

Henry And worse because I knew that for thirty-six years I should have loved you more than I did. I should have held you tighter. I should have loved you more.

The ghosts disappear. Eric and Henry are alone once again.

I can't change the past but I will not stare at it. I choose to close the door on it and leave it where it is. That is my right as someone who was there, as someone who survived. It is my right as someone who cannot close his eyes without seeing the faces of those he lost. If you cannot understand that, if you cannot accept that, if that is not enough for you, then I will release you from this marriage. I've only ever wanted to protect you, Eric. But I can only do that in the way I know how.

A moment, then Eric tentatively reaches to Henry, who takes his hand, holding it.

End of Scene One.

SCENE TWO

1. Beach on Fire Island

The sound of waves. A full moon shines brightly. Leo sits in the sand, watching the waves.

A figure enters, walking along the shore. He stops, sees Leo. It is Morgan.

Morgan You're out late. Or are you up early?

Leo Both, I guess. You want to join me?

Morgan I probably shouldn't. What would the other characters think? If Toby found out, we'd never hear the end of it.

Leo He won't be up for hours.

Morgan sits down next to Leo. They look out at the ocean, the moon shining in their faces.

Morgan Beautiful night.

Leo I never want to leave here. I love the moon, I love this beach, I love our house, I love Toby. I probably shouldn't. I *know* I shouldn't. I don't think that's going to end well.

Morgan Well, if it's any consolation, no love affair does.

Leo Some do.

Morgan In books, perhaps. In actual romance, there is no such thing as a happy ending. Whether by death or dissolution, to fall in love is to make an appointment with heartbreak.

Leo Ugh, maybe I should just read about it instead.

Morgan No, you should experience it for yourself, heartbreak and all.

Leo Were you ever in love?

Morgan I was. More than once. It was not love in the way you might recognize. But it was love to me.

Leo I learned how to fuck when I was fourteen but no one ever explained to me how to love.

Morgan So many of us were never given a healthy example of what it means to be homosexual. Which means, of course, no one ever taught us how to be ourselves, how to love, how to accept love. We couldn't find it in our cultures and so we had to find it in each other. Clandestinely, fearfully. And sometimes joyfully. Our educations occurred in parks, in public toilets, on these very dunes of Fire Island. Or Hampstead Heath, busier than Oxford Street on some summer nights. It was all dangerous and forbidden and furtive and wonderful. And along the way we hurt each other. Sometimes we caused each other great pain.

Leo Maurice and Alec never hurt each other.

Morgan That's because I ended my story before they could.
  Does the name Edward Carpenter mean anything to you?

Leo No.

Morgan That is regrettable if unsurprising. Edward Carpenter was a Victorian-era poet, philosopher, and one-time Anglican priest. He lived in the English countryside with his husband George Merrill. Of course, they didn't use that word to describe their relationship but theirs was a true marriage. I visited them in 1912 and you cannot know what it was like at that time to encounter two men living together openly, happily, as a couple. By this time, I was thirty-three and, while I knew that I was homosexual, I had still never touched another man with desire. The

241

day was getting on and Merrill invited me into the kitchen to help him prepare the dinner. As we talked, ever so deftly, Merrill reached over and touched me, feeling me at the roundest part of my buttock.

Leo He came on to you?

Morgan He made a play. I'd never been touched like that before. It unleashed a creative spring in me unlike any I'd ever felt. Who knew that my creative forces were to be located just north of my buttocks?

It was in that instant that I conceived the whole of *Maurice*. I wanted to capture what I saw, to write a simple love story about two ordinary affectionate men. I wanted it to be as revolutionary as Carpenter and Merrill's relationship. And it was imperative that it have a happy ending. The newspapers were filled with too many stories that ended with a young lad dangling from a noose or carted off to prison for his nature. I was determined to change that narrative, at least in fiction. Writing *Maurice* was the most terrifying, and the most exhilarating thing I had ever done. Hiding it from the world was the most shameful. My greatest regret is that I never lived to understand the impact that it had on people's lives. If I had even an inkling that you needed to read it as badly as I needed to write it, I might have been braver. But you have shown me that my book was then, as you are now, a link in this chain of gay men teaching one another, loving one another, hurting one another, understanding one another. This inheritance of history, of community, and of self. And from where you sit on this beach today, you have no idea whose lives you will touch, and which ones you will save. But in order to do that, you must love. Even though you know that your heart will be broken by it. The only way to heal heartache is to risk more.

Silence a moment.

Leo Will my story have a happy ending?

Morgan It is only in telling our stories, in living our lives, that we can answer that question. You have already lived quite a lifetime in your nineteen years. Far more than I had when I was your age. I think you are a remarkable person. And I suspect there is the smallest part of you that thinks so too. Perhaps you have more to say than you know.

Silence a moment.

Time for you to continue your story.

Leo Not yet.

Morgan Leo wakes from his dream.

Leo No.

Morgan He is not on Fire Island, he is not with E. M. Forster.

Leo Morgan, please.

Morgan He is back in Toby's apartment, back in Toby's bed.

Leo Leo reaches for Toby.

Morgan But Toby is not there. Leo attempts to remember the events of the night before:

Leo Leo and Toby in a taxi headed upstate. A beautiful wedding.

Morgan But an ugly scene.

Leo Toby's ex, screaming at them.

Morgan And then Leo remembers:

Leo Henry.
Leo calls out for Toby –

Morgan But he gets no answer.

Leo He goes to the living room, expecting to find Toby asleep on the sofa –

Morgan But instead, Leo finds a note in Toby's messy handwriting:
    'Leo –
    I'm sorry I left without saying goodbye.'

Leo No.

Morgan 'Please take any books you want. Most of them are yours anyway.'

Leo Toby . . .

Morgan 'I wish I were the man you think I am. You don't need me. In fact, you'll be better off without me.
    Here's five hundred dollars. It's all I could withdraw at this hour.
    xo,
    Toby.'

And with that, Toby Darling vanished from Leo's life as unexpectedly as he entered it. Also alone that autumn was Eric Glass.

    Eric enters.

Morgan Eric and Henry had been married for two months. But Eric saw little of his husband in that time. Henry was always off on one business trip of another, never home long enough for their relationship to put down roots.

Eric Eric wished he had Walter there to ask him about Henry. He wished Walter had told him more about their relationship, how to navigate Henry's silences and distances.

Morgan Eric would open drawers and closets whenever they visited Henry's Dutchess County estate –

Eric – as if searching for evidence of his predecessor.

Morgan But Eric found nothing. Not even a photograph. It was as if the past had been erased as thoroughly from the world as it had been from Henry's mind. As thoroughly as Toby had been erased from Leo's life. Both Eric and Leo were left to face the future alone.

Morgan exits, leaving Eric and Leo alone.

End of Scene Two.

SCENE THREE

Christmas Eve, 2017

1. David Koch Theater

Young Man 7 Eric Glass was now thirty-five years old.

Young Man 8 Not exactly a young man –

Young Man 5 – but not yet a middle-aged man.

Eric He was, quite simply, a man.

Young Man 6 He certainly possessed all the markers of adulthood. In fact, he was able to enumerate them:

Eric One husband.

Young Man 3 One personal trainer.

Young Man 4 One pilates instructor.

Young Man 5 One favorite yoga instructor.

Young Man 8 One primary care physician.

Young Man 7 One dentist.

Young Man 2 One allergist.

Young Man 3 One townhouse in the West Village.

Young Man 4 One two-hundred-acre property in Dutchess County.

Young Man 5 One ten-acre farmhouse further upstate (empty, used for storage).

Young Man 6 One pied-a-terre in London (Mayfair).

Young Man 7 And one in Paris (the 11th arrondissement).

Eric And, if he were to be absolutely technical about it, two stepsons and two daughters-in-law.

Young Man 6 Eric Glass was an adult.

Eric And yet, on occasion, Eric would wake in the night to the fear that his life was amounting to nothing, and that his days were accumulating as inconsequentially as autumn snow. He would lull himself back to sleep by reminding himself that he was loved, that he was protected, that he was fortunate. And that, he knew, was far more than most people could say.

Young Man 3 Christmas Eve arrived and with it, Eric's annual visit with his friends to *The Nutcracker*. Their seats had been upgraded to Prime Orchestra as an early Christmas present from Henry.

Eric Henry, you're going to love this –

Young Man 3 Unfortunately, Henry could not attend because he was called away with an urgent business matter.

Eric Oh. Well, Eric and Jasper . . .

Young Man 7 Jasper did not join them that year. He had not spoken to Eric in months.

Eric Well, the Jasons arrived –

Young Man 2 The Jasons also begged off, traveling instead to visit family in Pennsylvania for their new son's –

Young Man 8 – first Christmas!

Eric Eric stood by himself in the lobby, waiting for Tristan to arrive.

Young Man 4 The first act bell rang.

Young Man 3 The crowd moved into the auditorium, and Eric stood alone with his two tickets.

Young Man 5 When finally . . .

Tristan enters.

Tristan Hey, baby. Sorry I'm late. I've been on the phone with my mother all morning. Shall we go in?

Eric Is everything okay?

Tristan Yes, never better.

Eric You're a terrible liar. You know that, right?

Tristan We can talk after the show.

Eric Oh no, what? Now you have to tell me. Is she okay?

Tristan takes a breath.

Tristan I told her this morning that I'm moving to Canada in the new year. See? I told you you didn't want to have this conversation right now. Let's go back / into the –

Eric What are you talking about?

Tristan They're offering visas and fast-track citizenship to medical professionals willing to work in under-served areas.

Eric I . . . I don't even know what to say.

Tristan I know, this is huge, and they're ringing the bell. We can talk about this after the show.

Eric No, Tristan, please. Why are you moving to Canada?

Tristan I've been thinking about it a while now.

Eric For how long?

Tristan Since the election.

Eric Tristan.

Tristan This whole year has been . . . well . . .
  Eric, this country is destroying itself. And I can't stick around to watch it happen.

Eric But Tristan, you're an American.

Tristan No, Eric. I'm a gay, HIV-positive black man who lives in America. There is no place for me in this country anymore. I don't think there ever was. The last eight years were like a fantasy. But this year has shown us who we really are. And it is ugly. Much uglier than I ever thought.

Eric Do you really feel that way?

Tristan Honestly? It feels like America is reenacting the last thirty minutes of *Titanic* in slow motion – only in this version, they've rammed the boat directly at the iceberg. I ain't drowning for this fucking country. I'm gonna be Kathy Bates, watching the carnage from the safety of my lifeboat.

Eric Do you know how cynical that sounds? What about the people in this country who don't have that option? What about your patients?

Tristan Eric . . . you married a billionaire that you don't love. You're floating in a gold-plated lifeboat. The rest of us are not as safe as you.

Eric But this country needs people like you, Tristan.

The Nutcracker *Overture starts.*

Tristan This country doesn't deserve people like me. I don't owe this country a goddamned thing. America isn't worth saving anymore.

But I am.

The bell rings once again. Tristan exits, leaving Eric alone.

End of Scene Three.

SCENE FOUR

Winter 2018

1. Free Clinic

Leo waits in an exam room.

A Clinic Worker enters. He is harried, his mind on a million different things. He sorts through the files in his hands.

Clinic Worker Okay, you are . . . Jeff. No. Danny. No. Leo? Yes. Leo. So what's up, Leo?

Leo I have this cough.

Clinic Worker Is that all you came in wearing?

Leo Um. Yeah?

Clinic Worker It's February. No scarf, no coat?

Clinic Worker starts looking through Leo's file.

We don't have an address for you. Where are you living?

Leo Around.

Clinic Worker Got a working phone?

Leo Not right now.

He goes into a coughing fit.

Clinic Worker All right, have a seat.

*He indicates Leo should take his sweater off. Leo does.
Clinic Worker inspects Leo's arms.*

Leo I don't shoot up.

Clinic Worker Maybe not, but you do have bed-bug
bites. Okay, let's have a listen. Deep breath. You smoke
cigarettes?

Leo Sometimes.

Clinic Worker Pot? Breathe.

Leo Sometimes.

Clinic Worker Anything else?

No answer.

I can't treat you if you don't tell me everything. Crystal?

Leo Sometimes.

Clinic Worker How often?

Leo shrugs.

Once more.

*Leo takes a deep breath and falls into a fit of coughing.
Clinic Worker starts writing out prescriptions.*

Clinic Worker You've got bronchitis. If you'd waited any
longer it might have turned into pneumonia. I'm putting
you on a Z-Pak, plus some steroids and an inhaler. Okay,
let's talk about your HIV treatment.

Leo You mean PREP?

Clinic Worker PREP? No. I'm talking about your
antiretroviral treatment.

Leo For what?

Clinic Worker For your HIV.

Leo My – No, I'm not . . .

Clinic Worker That's not what this says.

Leo I . . .

Clinic Worker On your last visit . . . in November . . .
your bloodwork came back positive for HIV antibodies.
This is news to you?

Leo That's not possible.

Clinic Worker Why isn't it possible? No one called you?

Leo I . . .

Clinic Worker (*consulting the file*) We left a ton of
messages. You never called back or came in for a follow-
up.

Leo is silent.

You didn't know you were HIV positive?

*Leo sits there in shocked silenced. The phone rings.
Clinic Worker answers it. As he talks, Leo sits there
silently freaking out.*

What?
No, I can't.
I'm sorry. I've got plans tonight. I'm not even supposed
to be here today, I . . . Fine, but I'm definitely putting in
for overtime.

He hangs up.

Fucking ridiculous.

He turns his attention back to Leo.

We need to take more blood, check your viral load. How
many sexual partners have you had in the last six months?

No response from Leo.

Hey, uh . . . (*Looks down at the file.*) Leo. Sexual partners.

Leo I don't know.

Clinic Worker Ballpark it.

Leo Fifty?

Clinic Worker Do you have anyone you can call right now for support?

Leo shakes his head 'no'. Phone rings again. Clinic Worker answers angrily.

I'm coming!

He slams down the phone.

Are you sure there's no one you can call?

2. *The Streets*

Leo Leo left the clinic and wandered the frozen streets. He attempted a mental list of all the men he'd had sex with in the last six months, either for money, for shelter, for drugs. Never for pleasure. And of all the men at the parties in The Pines. Which of the nameless strangers had it been? Leo thought of the chain of infection that had been passed down along the years, decades and generations, his particular lineage moving from person to person, until it was eventually passed to him. A bitter inheritance. And yet, despite this chain of humanity, Leo never felt so alone in all his life.

And so Leo found himself walking in the direction of the last place he remembered being happy, the last place he remembered feeling safe. He approached Toby's doorman.

3. *Toby's Building*

Doorman Yes? What do you want?

Leo Is Toby home? Toby Darling?

Doorman And you are . . . ?

Leo I used to . . . Do you remember me?

Doorman No.

Leo Is Toby here?

Doorman I can't tell you that.

Leo Will you buzz up to him for me?

Doorman Is he expecting you?

Leo No.

Doorman I'm afraid I can't bother him.

Leo I need to see him.

Doorman You could always call him.

Leo Can I use your phone?

Doorman I'm afraid I can't let you do that.

Leo Can I . . . can I at least leave him a message?

Doorman begrudgingly hands Leo a pen and a piece of paper.

Leo didn't know what to write.

Young Man 8 'Help me, Toby, I'm in trouble'?

Young Man 5 'Find me, Toby, I'm lost'?

Young Man 7 'Comfort me, Toby, I'm afraid'?

Eric enters.

Doorman Yes, sir. Can I help you?

253

Eric I'm here to see Toby Darling. He's in, um . . . (*Checking his phone.*) 67C.

Leo looks up.

Doorman She's also looking for Toby Darling.

Eric and Leo lock eyes. Leo hands the note to the Doorman.

Leo Thank you.

He starts to leave.

Eric Oh. You're –
No – please, wait.
Leo?

Leo stops.

Your name is Leo, right?

Leo nods.

I'm Eric.

Leo I know.

Eric Listen, Leo . . . I came here to see Toby. I haven't heard from him since . . . since the wedding.

Leo That's the last time I saw him, too.

Eric Oh.
Do you know where he went?

Leo No. He just . . . disappeared.

Eric (*to the Doorman*) I need you to take me up to Toby's apartment.

Doorman I can't do that.

Eric I'm afraid that something might be wrong. I want to go up to his apartment and see. Can't you let me do that?

Doorman I'd have to call the building manager.

Eric Or I could call 9-1-1 and the police can break down the door. Maybe that'll be faster.

A moment, then . . .

Doorman All right, I'll take you up.

Eric Thank you.

Leo I want to come up, too.

Doorman No.

Leo He's my boyfriend.

Doorman Ugh, not while I'm eating!

Eric takes out his wallet, removes some cash and hands it to the Doorman.

Eric Now can we please go upstairs?

Young Man 5 They rode up the elevator in silence.

Young Man 7 Eric stole glances at Leo, knowing that the two most important men in his life had both had sex with him.

Young Man 8 Fighting his anger at the young man.

Young Man 7 Fighting his resentment.

Young Man 6 Knowing it was childish of him.

Leo They stepped into the apartment, where Leo had once been so happy.

4. *Toby's Apartment*

The Doorman unlocks the door and Eric and Leo walk inside.

Leo Nothing's been touched since I was here last. Look –

Leo picks up Toby's note.

He left this the night he disappeared.

>*Eric takes the note, reads it.*
>   *Leo moves to a stack of books in the corner, starts looking through them.*

Doorman Don't touch those.

Leo These are my books.

Doorman Those are Mr Darling's books.

Eric (*to the Doorman*) Okay, I think you can go now.

Doorman I can't just leave you here.

Eric (*slipping him more money*) Yes you can.

Doorman Lock the door behind you.

>*He exits. A beat, then:*

Eric He said nothing to you about where he was going?

Leo All he left was that note.

>*He has a coughing fit.*

Eric Are you okay?

Leo I'm fine.

Eric Do you need any help or –

Leo I need Toby.

Eric Are you hungry? Do you need –
    Do you want to come home with me? For dinner, maybe?

Leo I don't think your husband would like that.

>*A moment, then Eric then grabs a duffle bag and raids Toby's dresser, pulling out sweaters and thick woolen socks. He stuffs them into the duffle bag.*

Leo What are you doing?

Eric Helping you.

Leo I can't take / Toby's clothes.

Eric He doesn't need them.

He takes out his wallet, pulls out some cash.

Here . . .

Leo Please stop.

Eric Now I wish I hadn't bribed that guy so much. Take it.

Leo doesn't move.

Leo I don't want your money.

Eric Please let me help you.

Leo Will that make you feel better?

Eric Yes.

Leo takes Eric's money.

Leo Happy?

Eric goes to the book Leo had been holding a moment before. He picks it up, looking at it.

Eric *Maurice.* I used to love this book. If it's yours, you should take it.

He offers Leo the book. Leo takes it.

Leo Thank you.

5. Henry and Eric's Townhouse

Young Man 8 Eric returned home, where Henry and his son Charles were preparing for a business trip to Saudi Arabia.

Eric Hello, husband.

Henry I'll be with you in just a minute, Eric.

Charles So the Saudis have just sent yet another agreement.

Henry Oh Christ, what now?

Charles They're now insisting we borrow money from their banks in order to service the fees that they've just added to the lease agreement.

Henry In essence, they want us to borrow money from them in order to pay them the bribe they just demanded. It is, without question, the most breathtaking corruption I have ever encountered. You have to admire it.

Charles The guys at Skadden are looking it over.

Henry I want to read it myself on the flight. Charles, these plans they just sent over are all wrong. I want the architects on the flight. Get them to the airport now.

Charles They're already there. Honestly, Pop – this additional agreement is going to add at least another week to the trip.

Henry's Assistant enters, a stack of shirts in his hand.

Henry's Assistant Should I pack two more suits just in case?

Henry Just one. (*To Charles.*) It'll only add three days, tops.

Eric Henry, I cannot believe you make your assistant pack your clothes for you.

Henry How else do you think it gets done?

Eric It's just – surely that's not what he went to Harvard Business School to do.

Henry Harvard Business School is filled with young people who would be happy to pack my suits for me. (*To his Assistant.*) Isn't that right?

Henry's Assistant I beat out two hundred applicants for this job.

He exits.

Eric Henry, I –

Henry Just a minute, Eric. (*To Charles.*) Charles, I want you to call Deb Randolph at Morgan.

Charles I've already reached out to her.

Henry Good. Tell her we need her to guarantee another half-billion in financing, give or take.

Charles Yeah.

Henry But Charles, I do not want to pay those motherfuckers / any more than –

Charles We will get them down to no more than a quarter-billion.

Henry That's my boy.

Charles exits.

(*To Eric.*) How was your afternoon?

Eric Oh. Oh, fine.

Henry What'd you do?

Eric I finally got to see the Laura Owens exhibit at the Whitney.

Henry Hey, fantastic!

Charles enters.

Charles Paul's on the line. The plane's at Teterboro. We should go.

Henry Yeah, be right there.

Charles exits.

Eric Henry, how much money do you have?

Henry I've probably got a couple hundred on me, why?

Eric No, I mean net worth.

Henry That's a complicated answer.

Eric Well, let's say you had to pay a ransom and the kidnappers told you to give them all the money you had available. How much would you pay?

Henry That depends on who's been kidnapped.

Eric Let's say it was me.

Henry I've probably got a couple hundred on me.
    How much money, exactly, are you planning to spend while I'm away?

Eric No, I'm not asking for myself.

Henry Who are you asking for, then?

A beat.

Eric Well, when I worked for Jasper, I did something I cared about. And it wasn't just for me, it was, you know, for the greater good.

Henry And how does my net worth come to play in all this?

Eric Well, I was thinking I could do something with it. A part of it.

Henry You mean philanthropy?

Eric Yeah, maybe.

Henry I'm not going to let you spend my money empowering dyslexic pygmy hemp farmers through yoga and positive reinforcement.

Eric Well, obviously they'd have to be *organic* pygmy hemp farmers.

Henry Forgive me.

Eric I was thinking something a little less cartoonishly lefty than that.

Henry For instance?

Eric For instance . . . I follow a guy on Instagram who collects old winter coats and goes around the city giving them to any homeless people he encounters. I could support him.

Henry How?

Eric I could buy him a lot of coats.

Henry That's not philanthropy, that's charity.

Eric I doubt that a homeless person would quibble.

Henry You could also just give a homeless person twenty thousand dollars with which to rent and furnish an apartment.

Eric That sounds even better.

Henry Yes, I'm sure it does. But that's not how you solve homelessness.

Eric It would solve someone's homelessness.

Henry Yes, but you need to think big picture when you're talking philanthropy. You can't get bogged down in minutiae.

The Assistant re-enters.

Henry's Assistant Do you want me to pack the Brioni or the Kiton lightweight wool?

Henry I couldn't care less.

Henry's Assistant The Kiton, then.

He starts to exit when –

Henry The Brioni.

The Assistant exits.

(*To Eric.*) What's brought all this on?

Eric hesitates. Then –

Is it because I'm leaving?

Eric No.

Charles re-enters.

Charles Plane's on the runway, Pop. We should go.

Henry Thank you, Charles.

Charles exits.

Eric Listen, Henry – there's / something –

Henry If it were any other place in the world –

Eric I know, Henry –

Henry American businessmen cannot bring their husbands with them to Saudi Arabia.

Eric I understand.

Henry I'll only be gone six weeks. The time will fly by, I promise.

Eric Yes.

Henry exits.

Eric watched Henry disappear out the door when an urge overcame him and, before he could fight it, he called Toby, immediately getting his voicemail:

Listen, Toby, I don't know where you are. I hope you're okay. I went to your apartment today, hoping

I might find you there. I saw Leo. He was looking for you, too. Toby, he's not well. He isn't at all well, in fact, and I –

Just call me when you can.

End of Scene Four.

SCENE FIVE

Spring 2018

1. Various Locations

Leo Leo wakes next to a man he doesn't know in a room he doesn't recognize in a bed he can't remember lying down in.

Young Man 6 Panic seizes him as he searches his body for any signs of disorder.

Young Man 7 He checks for blood –

Leo – none.

Young Man 2 For cuts –

Leo – a few.

Young Man 4 For new scratches and for old scars –

Leo – yeah, both.

Young Man 6 He then goes about inspecting its internal condition.

Young Man 7 Head fuzzy and pounding –

Leo – yeah, common.

Young Man 2 Mouth stale and cottony –

Leo – okay, normal.

263

Young Man 4 Stomach empty –

Leo – fuckin' always.

Young Man 3 Heart pounding –

Leo – more than usual.

Young Man 8 Anus slick with lubricant –

Leo – also normal.

Young Man 2 Teeth . . . ah, the teeth.

Young Man 6 That's a new development.

Young Man 2 They wobble at the slightest encounter with food –

Young Man 4 – which admittedly is a rare occurrence these days.

Leo He knows they'll eventually fall out.

Young Man 8 If the malnutrition doesn't get them, the meth certainly will.

Young Man 6 Meth.

Young Man 5 Crystal.

Young Man 4 Tina.

Young Man 2 A currency in a world he's descended to, just as his body has become a currency.

Leo Does he sell his body to tweak or does tweaking cause him to sell his body?

Young Man 6 Chicken and egg, really.

Leo Ugh, the thought of food makes his stomach heave. He hasn't eaten in . . . well, who knows what day it is?

Young Man 8 Leo looks down at the man lying next to him.

Young Man 6 Revulsion bubbles up from the part of him that still cares.

Young Man 7 Has he told this man about his status? That he is HIV positive and detectable?

Leo Detectable. That's the last thing Leo has ever felt in his life. His viral load is the only part of him that registers in the world.

Young Man 5 Leo stands and looks for his clothes, the clothes he's been living in for weeks.

Young Man 3 They reek.

Leo But Leo knows that the real stench comes from him.

Young Man 4 Leo reaches into his jacket pocket and finds his sole possession . . . his battered paperback copy of *Maurice*.

Leo He can't read it anymore because he can't make sense of the words.

Young Man 2 His malnourished, drug-addled brain is now just a simple processor of binary concepts: day/night –

Young Man 7 Sleep/wake –

Young Man 3 High/not high –

Leo Leo has forgotten how to read.

Young Man 6 Leo glances at the kitchen. The man's wallet rests on the counter, tantalizingly unguarded.

Young Man 5 Multiple twenty-dollar bills blossom from the opening like the meat inside a shell or the fruit inside a husk.

Young Man 8 Shell.

Young Man 7 Husk.

Young Man 3 That is all he is now.

Leo But of all the things he's become . . .

Young Man 8 Whore –

Young Man 7 Addict –

Young Man 3 Transmitter of plague –

Leo . . . Is he also a thief?

Young Man 6 Take the money. You need it.

Leo Leo reaches for the wallet –

Young Man 8 – and his eyes land on a jar of peanut butter. He grabs it, making a beeline for the door –

Young Man 4 – not stopping until it closes behind him, a barrier between him and the money.

Young Man 8 Leo is not a thief.

Young Man 4 Then he looks down at the purloined jar in his hand and revises his assessment:

Leo Leo is not *much* of a thief.

Young Man 4 He steps out into the thin light.

Leo Morning or evening?

Young Man 4 Where is the sun?

Leo Over the Hudson.

Young Man 4 Evening, then. It's pleasant out. Springtime now.

Leo Six months since Toby abandoned him.

Young Man 4 Leo turns toward the river with his dinner. He opens the jar of peanut butter.

Young Man 8 He digs his dirty, sex-smelling fingers into the jar, scooping up a giant mouthful and stuffing it into his gob.

Young Man 4 Pleasure instantly overtakes him.

Young Man 8 He even smiles.

Young Man 5 Even his unhappy childhood cannot erase the pleasures of peanut butter: the gentle touch of his mother's hand on his shoulder, imploring him to eat his sandwich slower.

Young Man 2 His mother, who was the first person to visit her anger and frustrations on the boy.

Young Man 3 For being born.

Young Man 7 For requiring affection.

Young Man 6 For driving away boyfriend after boyfriend by his mere existence.

Young Man 5 And then, later, for attracting their unwanted attention.

Young Man 2 Leo wasn't sure when he and his mother became competitors for the affections of these men.

Young Man 4 It was never something he initiated or sought.

Young Man 2 The trysts . . .

Young Man 4 No, the assaults.

Young Man 2 The assaults occurred while his mother worked the dinner shift.

Young Man 4 They were violations, he knew.

Young Man 8 They certainly weren't acts of love.

Leo And yet he had begun to allow himself to believe they were.

Young Man 5 By the time he was fourteen, Leo grew flagrant, audacious. He realized his body was not to be traded away cheaply.

Leo The day his mother discovered Leo and her boyfriend deep into their rut, she kicked out the boyfriend and Leo as well.

Young Man 7 The man gave Leo forty dollars and his first case of chlamydia.

Young Man 3 A week later Leo was in New York.

Young Man 6 He was seventeen years old.

Leo And now here he is, three years later, eating peanut butter for dinner with no place to go and no one to go to. This is what his life has amounted to. And he thinks to himself: what will become of me? How much longer will I live? Do I even care to live anymore?

This seems to alarm the Lads.

Young Man 4 He wonders what Forster might say about his current state.

Leo But then Leo remembers that E. M. Forster is dead. And all Leo has of him is one book.

Young Man 5 And, like Leo, that book has started to disintegrate.

Young Man 6 The only difference is that *Maurice* would be remembered and Leo would not.

Leo And, Leo thinks, if that is the case, what's the fucking point of all this suffering? Why go on if no one cares and no one ever will?

Young Man 4 Leo crosses Eighth Avenue –

Leo – and remembers that a hundred blocks north lies the George Washington Bridge –

Young Man 2 – the final resort for so many negations like himself.

Leo Leo turns north and heads toward the bridge, ready to write the end of his story.

Young Man 6 No, he keeps going east.

Young Man 5 Along 46th Street.

Young Man 3 To Toby's theatre.

Leo No.

Young Man 4 Yes. That is what he does.

Leo No, he goes to the fucking bridge.

Young Man 4 Leo goes to Toby's theatre.

Leo No, I can't. Please.

Young Man 3 Leo turns in the direction of Toby's theatre.

Young Man 8 Leo turns in the direction of Toby's theatre.

Young Man 2 Leo turns in the direction of Toby's theatre.

Leo PLEASE DON'T MAKE ME GO ON LIKE THIS!!

Young Man 4 Leo turns in the direction of Toby's theatre to remember, for a moment, his life before Toby left him.

Leo The time that Leo was happy.

Young Man 4 The time that Leo was loved.

A moment, then:

Leo Leo stands in front of the theatre. Emblazoned across the doors are enormous photos of Adam. Leo studies Adam's face, so robust and healthy, his eyes bright with intelligence and hope. Leo stares at Adam's picture and sees how beautiful Adam is. And he knows how ugly he is. And he thinks once again about the bridge.

Young Man 5 And then a voice behind him:

Adam Are you okay? Do you need help?
Hey. What's your name?

Leo I'm Leo.

Adam Hi Leo. I'm Adam.

Leo I know. Your name is Adam McDowell. And everybody loves you.

Adam Do you need help, Leo?

Leo Yeah. I need help.

Adam What do you need? Is there someone I can call for you?

Leo Eric.

Adam I'm sorry, what? I can't hear you.

Leo Eric.

Adam Eric? Eric who, Leo?

Leo Eric.
   Glass.

Adam Did you say 'Eric Glass'? How do you know Eric?

Leo Eric was kind to me.

Adam He was kind to me, too. Do you want me to call Eric for you, Leo?

Leo Yes.

Adam Okay, Leo. I'll call him right away.

Leo starts to cry. His knees buckle and he wobbles to the ground. Adam catches him and eases him down.

Leo Please help me. I'm sorry. I'm sorry.

Adam It's okay, Leo. It's okay.

Young Man 3 Two strangers kneeling on the dirty sidewalk, clinging to each other as one of them weeps, creating an obstruction in the path of the people heading toward the theatre to see Adam McDowell perform in Toby's play. A performance that had made Adam a star and, on this night, a performance he would miss.

2. *Adam Lucas McDowell*

Eric Adam delivered Leo to Eric and Henry's townhouse. Eric fed the young man –

Young Man 8 Chicken broth and toast.

Eric Gave him a shower.

Young Man 4 Expensive soap, French shampoo.

Eric He gave Leo a clean T-shirt and pajama bottoms.

Young Man 7 J.Crew shirt, GAP pajamas.

Eric He put Leo up in a guest room to sleep.

Young Man 6 Thousand-thread-count bedsheets.

Young Man 1 Eric and Adam, who had once meant so much to each other, caught up in each other's lives.

Adam What will happen to him?

Eric I don't know. I'll take him to a doctor in the morning and we'll see.

Adam I'm sorry to drop all this on you. Especially when we haven't seen each other in so long.

Eric You did the right thing. I'll take care of him.

Adam I think a lot about that summer we spent together. It feels like a lifetime ago. You know, I finally watched *Beau Travail*. I didn't really understand it. I wish I'd had you with me to explain it to me. I'm sorry that we lost touch, Eric. It's my fault. I got –

Eric (*with love*) Famous.

Adam Busy. Could I – could we have that friendship again? I didn't realize until just now how much I missed you.

Eric Yes. Yes, of course Adam. I would love that.

Adam You really are a remarkable man.

Eric No, I'm not remarkable.

Adam No, Eric: you are. How can you not know that?

His phone rings.

Oh shit, it's my producer calling.

Eric Take it.

Young Man 6 And yet, despite their promises to each other, Eric Glass and Adam McDowell would never see each other again after that night.

Young Man 5 Their lives would move in separate directions.

Young Man 7 Eric had come into his life when Adam was most in need of his friendship and he left it once Adam was ready to become the man that he would inevitably be.

Young Man 8 Someone else needed Eric now and Adam had delivered him to his old friend.

Young Man 4 The debt had been repaid.

3. Henry and Eric's Townhouse / A Hotel in Riyadh

Young Man 3 Eric called Henry in Riyadh.

Eric Something's happened that you need to know about.

Henry Are you okay?

Eric I'm fine.

Henry What's this about?

Eric It's about Leo.

Silence from Henry.

Henry? Are you there?

Henry What about him?

Eric He's asleep in our upstairs guest room.

Silence.

Henry?

Henry Why?

Eric He's been sleeping on the streets. He's sick, he's malnourished, and he's deep in the throes of addiction. And he has an untreated HIV infection.

Henry Is he saying I gave it to him?

Eric No, Henry.

Henry Has he come there to blackmail me?

Eric Henry, Leo hasn't come here to blackmail you or to accuse you of anything. He's come here asking for help.

Henry But why has he come to *me*?

Eric He hasn't, Henry, he's come to me.

Henry Where's Toby in all of this?

Eric Disappeared the night of our wedding. Leo hasn't heard from him in over six months. Henry, he's completely alone in the world.

Henry Well, ah, you should take him to a doctor.

Eric I plan to as soon as he's awake.

Henry Make sure he gets whatever he needs. And, ah, be sure to give him some money to help him get back on his feet.

Eric Henry, Leo needs our help, not just our assistance.

Henry What are you suggesting we do?

Eric I want him to stay with us / for a while.

Henry No.

Eric You'll be gone for the next five weeks.

Henry Eric, that is just not possible.

Eric Why isn't it possible?

Henry Because what you're describing is a months-perhaps even years-long undertaking.

Eric Who better than a billionaire to undertake it?

Henry He's not a stray dog you can just bring in off the street.

Eric You make it sound as though he's worse than that. We can't just fob him off with a few dollars and some kind words, Henry.

Henry You cannot sacrifice yourself to save him.

Eric Why can't I?

Henry Because he isn't our responsibility.

Eric You don't feel like we owe some kind of debt here?

Henry I never gave him drugs. I didn't make him sick.

Eric You and Toby treated him as if he were disposable.

Henry Do not compare me to Toby. Toby's the one who brought him to my house in six different kinds of altered states. He's the one you should be giving this lecture to / not me.

Eric You paid a nineteen-year-old boy to have sex with you! You don't get to take advantage of a desperate young

274

person when it suits you and then turn your back on him when it becomes inconvenient. Why can't you be honest with yourself for once in your life and say: 'What Toby has done, I have done too'?

Henry Am I responsible for every person I've ever fucked? Am I responsible for every person you've ever met? You cannot save the entire world, Eric.

Eric I'm only trying to save one person.

Henry Which person, Eric? Him or yourself? Get him the fuck out of my house.

4. *The Streets*

Eric Eric stormed out of the townhouse and into the streets of the West Village, raging at Henry's heartlessness. He was furious at Henry for confirming all of Jasper's dire warnings about him.

But Eric was also furious with himself. Eric had spent his life refusing to make waves because he knew that it was in them that the weakest swimmers drowned. When Toby left him, Eric had grabbed the nearest lifeboat and pulled himself to safety, leaving everyone else behind. And on that day in Toby's apartment, it was Eric who had fobbed Leo off with a few dollars and some kind words. Eric had chosen his own comfort over the needs of this frightened young man. And in realizing that, Eric understood that he was no mere witness to Leo's suffering. He was one of its authors.

Eric crossed Seventh Avenue and entered the park in Sheridan Square. Sitting on a bench in his expensive clothes, holding the keys to his thirty-million-dollar home, Eric Glass asked himself the simple questions:

'What good am I? To what use has my life been put?'

Eric glanced over at the Stonewall Inn, just across the square from where he sat, where, years before, an unexpected group of people roared their defiance at their powerlessness. Those people did not fear drowning. They built their own lifeboats. They saved themselves. No. They saved each other.

It was the same salvation that Walter had found. A salvation based on the understanding that the way to save the world was to first save one person.

Eric took a breath and looked around him.

What was the responsibility between gay men from one generation to another? What was Eric's role in that continuum? Eric wished he had Walter there with him to ask his advice, to seek his guidance. Walter would have known what to do.

And in that moment, Eric had his answer, as if Walter was still illuminating the path for him even now.

There is a house three hours north of the city that sits unloved and unused. A house that had once been a place where young men went to die. Maybe it could now be a place where they went to thrive.

End of Act Two.

Act Three

Spring 2018

SCENE ONE

1. A Hotel Room in Alabama

Young Man 3 Four forty-six in the morning,

Young Man 6 in the finest hotel room in the state of Alabama.

Young Man 4 The night Toby disappeared, he took the Acela to Richmond. The end of the line.

Young Man 8 He had left without a plan.

Young Man 6 It wasn't until the train was halfway to DC that he realized where he was going –

Young Man 2 – where his body had reflexively started to travel before his mind caught wind of the scheme.

Young Man 7 He got off the train, took a taxi to the nearest Honda dealership and bought a new Civic off the lot –

Young Man 5 – and drove through the night to his hometown in Alabama.

Toby 'Hometown'. It wasn't his hometown. Manhattan was his hometown.

Young Man 5 He knew where he was headed.

Young Man 4 Less so why.

Young Man 3 All he knew was that he had exhausted his options.

Young Man 6 He could move forward no longer.

Toby He thought of the explorers who first encountered the Grand Canyon. Their first thought must have been: 'Oh wow.' Their second: 'Aw fuck. How do I get around that thing?'

Young Man 8 Toby knows he's in a similar place –

Young Man 5 – and that there's no getting around it.

Young Man 4 There's only retreating back up the path –

Young Man – 2 no matter how long you've been traveling it –

Young Man 6 – until you reach the fork in the road where you made your first wrong decision –

Young Man 7 – where you went left –

Young Man 5 – when you should have gone right.

Young Man 8 Toby has to retrace his steps.

Young Man 3 And so here he is – four forty-six in the morning,

Young Man 6 in the finest hotel room in the state of Alabama.

Young Man 3 And so here he is – four forty-six in the morning –

Young Man 6 – in the finest hotel room in the state of Alabama.

Young Man 3 And so here he is . . .

Toby He was seven when his father died. Toby had been the one who discovered the body slumped in his leather desk chair, his brains splattered across the window behind him, as if yearning for a view of the Hudson River. Toby stared at his father's lifeless face, at his startled eyes staring back at him as if to say, 'Son, if ever you were curious, I would not recommend this particular escape route.' Toby heard doors slamming in his future that he barely understood to be open to him. He knew at that moment that he would be forever on his own. He knew, even at the age of seven, that he was well and truly fucked.

Young Man 5 Toby's mother / was born . . .

Toby His mother didn't come out of her room for days. Her only words to him at the funeral were, 'Chin up,' which he mistakenly heard as, 'Cheer up,' for which he resented her for the rest of her life. Not that 'Chin up' was exactly the stuff of wise, motherly direction but at least it had a 'pull yourself up by your bootstraps, we can survive this together' intimation. But 'cheer up', which is what Toby thought he heard, was unspeakably cruel. He knew in that moment he had lost the wrong parent.

Young Man 5 Toby's mother was born and raised in Alabama –

Toby – and very wisely escaped on her seventeenth birthday to become an actress and a model in New York.
   She met Toby's father before she had time to fail at both endeavors and they lived together, ensconced in wealth, access and privilege –

Young Man 4 – until the day his father ended his life –

Young Man 3 – leaving the family with nothing to its name.

Toby Not even his name, in fact, which they discovered had been appropriated from *Peter Pan*, his father's favorite childhood story. Toby, he was to discover in more ways than one, wasn't really Darling after all.

Young Man 5 Toby and his mother returned to her childhood home in Alabama –

Toby – a state he had never heard of, let alone visited.

Young Man 8 They lived there with his grandmother –

Toby – of whom the same could be said.

Young Man 7 Toby's mother lost herself in alcohol –

Toby – the way a convert loses themselves in religion.

Young Man 2 (Like mother, like son.)

Young Man 5 And then / Toby Darling was deposited . . .

Toby And then Toby Darling, the golden boy, raised in privilege, trained in the violin and in ballet, educated at the finest prep schools in Manhattan –

Young Man 5 Was deposited . . .

Toby – was deposited in an Alabama public school, where he was anything but a golden boy.

Young Man 7 Ostracized for his sensitivity –

Young Man 2 – for his scandalous interest in learning.

Young Man 3 Even the teachers mistrusted him.

Young Man 8 No one knew what to do with this sensitive –

Young Man 5 – effeminate –

Young Man 4 – sing-songy –

Young Man 6 – twinkle-toed –

Young Man 3 – wide-eyed –

Toby – broken-hearted child.

Young Man 2 It wasn't long before Toby's new schoolmates smelled the blood in the water.

Young Man 3 He was eight –

Toby Eight, when he was first called a faggot.

Young Man 5 Faggot.

Young Man 7 Faggot.

Toby He did not even know its meaning the first time it was hurled against him. He only knew it was not a good thing to be called. He could tell by the way it was flung off the snarling lips of the boy who first uttered it. The hatred in his eyes directed solely at Toby, the only one of his kind at school. The only faggot.

Young Man 5 Faggot.

Young Man 7 Faggot.

Toby Toby explored the word in his mind. The fricative beginning and the plosive ending. The glottal stop in between. It became his only possession in life. As Kevin Olson spits sunflower husks at his face on the bus. Toby sitting there petrified and helpless. Afraid to acknowledge what is happening to him. Afraid he'll cry if he does. The children around him laughing at the spectacle.

Young Man 5 Faggot.

Young Man 7 Faggot.

Young Man 4 Faggot.

Toby Toby traveling inward, into himself. He cannot protect his body so he hides inside his mind.

Young Man 5 Faggot.

Young Man 8 Faggot.

Young Man 6 Faggot.

Toby And returning home to a mother, once beautiful, now ugly from alcohol; to a grandmother, whose faith was no match for the despair that has filled her house; and to a poverty so crushing, he would sometimes go to school for days unwashed. How the boy seated next to him complained in front of the entire class that he could not concentrate because he could smell Toby's stinking asshole. Daily these assaults occurred and daily he was counseled to pray. For his tormentors, for himself. Pray for those who called him a faggot.

Young Man 5 Faggot.

Young Man 7 Faggot.

Toby Daily, Toby was sent unprotected into the world to be despised and abused at the hands of people far less worthy than he of God's love yet far more certain of their right to an outsized share of it. Every walk through town felt dangerous, every school day possessed the potential for violence. Toby would steal his mother's sleeping pills, hoarding them, planning his suicide. He would stare at them nightly, holding them in his hands, telling himself they were the pathway out of his pain, that they were more powerful than prayer.

Young Man 2 Like father, like son.

Toby Toby stared and stared at them until one night, perilously close to swallowing them, he was struck by the realization that –
   – that –
   – that he had not stolen enough. And that he would always live a life of scarcity, no matter how much he has.

Young Man 5 This is the world to which Toby Darling feels compelled to return –

Young Man 2 – now that he is an established –

Young Man 7 – successful –

Young Man 3 – yet no less lost young man.

Toby Because he knows he can never truly escape this place, his shame and humiliation.

Young Man 3 Nor can he escape the pain of Adam, who was an orphan like him –

Toby – but who, unlike him, was rescued.

Young Man 6 And Eric, who only ever wanted to love him –

Toby – something he knew Toby was never taught to accept or return.

Young Man 4 And Leo –

Silence.

Toby And so, four forty-six in the morning, in the finest hotel room in the state of Alabama, Toby faces a choice: can he accept, could he forgive, does he heal – or does he burn himself and everything around him to the ground? Heal or burn, those are his only choices. Heal and grow. Heal and seek truth, dignity and fulfillment. Heal and build a life that is real.

Young Man 7 Or burn it all –

Toby – his memories, his past, his anger, his pain, and ultimately himself.

Young Man 3 Heal or burn. Those are the only two options before him.

Toby And so in that room in that hotel in that town in Alabama, Toby finally looks at himself. And he sees who he is. And he knows that he must make a choice.

Young Man 3 Heal or burn, Toby.

Young Man 4 Heal or burn.

Toby It is a choice he has been running from his entire life.

Young Man 4 Can he accept his life for what it is, what it has been –

Young Man 3 – or will he reject his history, his story, and ultimately himself?

Young Man 5 Heal or burn, Toby.

Young Man 8 Heal or burn.

Toby And in that moment, Toby Darling knows what he must do.

Silence.

Toby Darling has to tell the truth. About himself, about his life. Toby Darling has to let himself be known to the world so that the world will finally accept Toby Darling for who he is. The boy who lost his parents, the boy who cried himself to sleep, the boy who smelled, the boy who was tormented, the boy who was never held, never comforted, the boy who was never loved, the boy who was never worthy of love. Toby Darling must tell the world how he became Toby Darling. And so, four forty-six in the morning, in the finest hotel room in the state of Alabama, Toby Darling starts to write.

Young Man 8 Toby's new play pours out of him in torrents.

Young Man 4 It is born of a creative urge so strong it hurts to keep inside his head.

Toby He labors over it for months, writing and rewriting it furiously in his hotel room in Alabama, barely keeping up with the words as they tumble from his mind.

Young Man 6 His work is fueled by Adderall and cocaine.

Young Man 3 His sleep is brokered by Ambien and alcohol.

Toby He calls the new play *Lost Boy*, which is intended as a follow-up to his hit play *Loved Boy*.

Young Man 5 A sequel?

Toby No, a rejection. This play contains all the truths of Toby's life. Things he spent years avoiding. Stories he should have told Eric. Pain he should have shared with Leo. For the first time in his life, Toby has written honestly. Toby sends it to his agent, gets into his car and drives through the night back to New York City.

2. *Agent's Office*

Agent So I read your play.

Toby And?

Agent I had my assistant circle all your typos.

Toby My typos?

Young Man 4 Here's a list of them by page.

Toby Is this a joke? A twenty-page list of my typos?

Young Man 4 You had a lot of typos.

Agent This script is over four hundred pages! You can't ask an audience to sit through a play that long!

Toby I can do some cutting.

Agent I think it's more than just cutting you need to do. Toby, this play just doesn't make any sense.

Toby That play is the best thing I've ever written.

Agent No, Toby. *Loved Boy* is the best thing you've ever written.

Toby No, *Loved Boy* was a lie. This is the truth.

Agent Nobody wants this depressing shit from you, Toby. It isn't your brand.

Toby Please. You don't understand what this play means to me. / I poured –

Agent You've been worrying me for a while, Toby, but reading this and seeing you like this right now – honestly, you're scaring the shit out of me.

Toby Okay, yeah, I've been a little checked out lately / but it's because I've been writing this play.

Agent Look, you need to understand that your reputation in this business is in the toilet right now. You get fired off your own play. Your director and your star refuse to even be in a room with you. You vanish for seven months. And now here you are, back from the dead, looking like shit, reeking of alcohol, and you dump this fifty-pound play on my desk and insist that I send it out.

Toby (*simultaneously, overlapping*)
    Look, I know I've been a little –
    But I really believe –
    I poured my –
    Oh, fuck Adam, he's irrelevant.
    You don't know what it –
    My heart, my heart and my fucking –
    I need, I need, I, I, I, I need to –
    I'll fucking die if I don't.
    I can't really think straight right now.

Please, listen to me. *Loved Boy* isn't my story, it isn't who I am.

Agent Then who are you, Toby?

Toby (*re: the new play*) There. That play is who I am.

Agent Well, there we are in agreement. Because both you and this script are an unintelligible mess / right now.

Toby Oh come on / there is good writing in there.

Agent This doesn't feel like the work of the man who wrote *Loved Boy*, it feels like the work of someone who hates the man / who wrote *Loved Boy*.

Toby There is truth in there. My life / is in there.

Agent I cannot in good conscience send this to anyone, Toby.

Toby Please, I have nothing left if I – I have to tell the truth.

Agent Then you need to admit that you've got a drug and alcohol problem.

Toby NO, I NEED YOU TO SEND OUT THIS PLAY!

Another Agent appears at the door.

Other Agent Hey Toby, good to see you.

Agent This is Alex. He works in our sports department.

Toby HI, ALEX!!

Other Agent Listen, I know this place in Pennsylvania. I went there seven years ago. It saved my life. Why don't we go get a cup of coffee and have a talk?

Toby Are you joking?

Agent We're worried about you, Toby.

Toby I'm not, I'm not going to a fucking rehab.

Agent We think maybe you should.

Toby I'm not – no – I don't – how dare you?

Agent We only want what's best for you, Toby.

Other Agent I have been where you are, man.

Toby No you haven't. I'm on top of the fucking world. You're a goddamned sports agent. Go fuck yourself. I'm not a – I don't need a –
Gimme my fucking play.

He grabs the printed manuscript.

Agent Toby, please don't do this.

Other Agent The first step is always the hardest, Toby.

Agent If you don't get help, we cannot continue to represent you.

3. *Toby's Apartment*

Toby Toby storms into his apartment and quickly drafts an email. Subject line: 'My new play'.

'My former agent refuses to send this out so I fired him and am doing it myself. It's the best thing I've ever written.'

Toby then opens his address book and copies every single person.

Young Man 2 Friends,

Young Man 4 Colleagues,

Young Man 7 Fellow writers,

Young Man 5 Agents,

Young Man 8 Literary managers,

Young Man 3 Artistic directors,

Young Man 4 Studio and network executives,

Young Man 7 Film producers,

Young Man 5 Broadway producers,

Young Man 6 *Times* reporters,

Young Man 2 Former lovers,

Young Man 8 Long-lost friends,

Young Man 4 His optometrist,

Young Man 3 Eric,

Young Man 6 Tristan,

Young Man 2 *and* **8** The Jasons,

Young Man 5 Tom Durrell,

Young Man 7 The cast of his play,

Young Man 6 Adam,

Toby *and* **Lads** Everyone.

Toby A voice inside him tells him to stop and think about this but before he has time to listen, Toby hits send.

Young Man 4 757 emails – going, going, going . . .

Toby And then that voice roars at him: 'STOP! Stop, Toby, for God's sake stop!' And Toby is snapped back to coherence. He reaches for the mouse pad and tries to stop the emails but they keep going.

Young Man 8 Five emails,

Young Man 2 Twenty,

Young Man 7 Fifty emails,

Young Man 6 One hundred.

Toby Toby tries to disengage the wi-fi but his trembling fingers won't obey his commands.

Young Man 5 Two hundred,

Young Man 3 Three hundred more emails.

Toby Toby starts to pound on the computer, trying desperately to stop the slow suicide he has just initiated upon his career.

Young Man 4 Five hundred emails sent.

Toby Toby screams. He picks up the computer and smashes it down on the ground.

Young Man 3 Texts and emails begin to pour in almost immediately.

Young Man 8 Toby, it this for real?

Young Man 7 Toby, are you okay?

Young Man 6 Toby, do you realize you sent this to a thousand people?

Young Man 4 Toby, I can't wait to read this.

Young Man 3 Toby, delete me from your contacts.

Young Man 2 Toby, where have you been?

Young Man 5 Toby, you just destroyed your career.

Eric Toby, did you mean to include me in this email? Are you okay? I've been trying to reach you. Call me. I'm going to Walter's house tomorrow. I think you should come and meet me there. I think there's a lot we both need to face.

Toby And then a voice in his head. A voice long dormant, now insisting: 'This is not the man you're meant to be. There is another way.'

End of Scene One.

SCENE TWO

Spring 2018

Eric And so Eric traveled once again to Walter's house. Eric tried to engage Leo in conversation but Leo barely uttered a word. Eric embraced the quiet, taking his time with the drive, opting for back roads over the thruway. He powered off his phone, trusting his memory of the drive he had taken the year before. They were lost within minutes. But the day was beautiful and Leo smiled as he breathed in the country air through his rattling lungs. As the farmland of upstate rolled past them, Eric could feel a release in Leo's body. They eventually found the house – a place at which Eric had preciously spent less than an hour. Eric was almost instantly struck with fear that he had jumped into the water without first measuring its depth. Eric was terrified. And, strangely, he felt more like himself than he had in years.

1. Walter's House

Eric and Leo approach the house. Leo takes in the house, the property.

Leo You own this house?

Eric No. It belongs to my –
It used to belong to a friend of mine. His name was Walter. Walter loved this house. He wanted so much to share it with me but he never got a chance. You and I can explore it together, once you're up for it.

He breathes deeply.

Smell that air. So sweet and clean.

Eric takes a deep breath. Leo follows suit, then falls into a coughing fit.

Okay. We can try that again later.

He places a comforting arm around Leo.

You will get better.

Leo That's hard for me to believe right now.

Eric I know. It probably won't be easy. But I will help you try. I promise.

Leo looks out at the meadow.

Leo Those wildflowers are beautiful.

Eric They are, aren't they? You know what? I'll be right back.

He runs off toward the meadow.

The breeze picks up. Leo closes his eyes and feels it on his face. The sounds of birds and rustling trees and, distantly, a wind chime. While his eyes are still closed, A Woman appears. Her name is Margaret. She's in her seventies. She watches Leo a moment. Then:

Margaret Hello.

Leo jumps, startled.

I didn't mean to startle you. You looked very peaceful just then. You can't be Eric.

Leo No, I'm Leo.

Margaret I'm Margaret. Is Eric with you?

Leo He's picking flowers in the meadow.

Margaret stares off in Eric's direction, as if studying him.

Margaret What do we think of him?

Leo Eric? He's nice.

Margaret Is he? That's good to know. Any other adjectives you'd care to use?

Leo He's kind. Gentle. Honest.

Margaret I like those kinds of people.

Leo I don't know many.

Margaret That's because there aren't many.
You picked a beautiful day.

Leo It's peaceful here.

Margaret I think so.

Leo I still have the city in my head. Car horns and chaos.

Margaret That'll fade eventually. I understand you're unwell.

Leo Eric thinks I'll get better here.

Margaret Do you think you will?

Leo I don't know anymore.

Margaret I know you will. If that is of any comfort. Come here. There's something I want to show you.

Leo hesitates, then takes her hand, slowly rising. She leads him to the cherry tree.

This tree is over four hundred years old, can you imagine that?

Local histories of this area include stories about this tree. Stories that stretch as far back as the colonial days.

Leo Are those . . . teeth?

Margaret Good eye. Those are pig's teeth. They've been embedded there for centuries.

Leo Why?

Margaret Well, it was once believed that chewing the bark of this tree can cure toothaches and other maladies.

Leo No.

Margaret That's the legend.

Leo Can it?

Margaret If only it were that easy. But no, of course it doesn't. That's just superstition. The colonists who arrived here from England brought them with them. The superstitions, that is. Not the teeth. Although perhaps both, who knows? What I do find remarkable about that story is that it proves that people have been coming to this place for centuries in search of healing. Like you have. If there's any consolation that I can give you, it is that you are not the first.

Leo looks up at the tree's branches and touches the trunk.
Eric enters, carrying a bundle of wildflowers in his hands.

Eric Hi. Are you / Margaret?

Margaret Margaret Avery, yes.

Eric Margaret, hello. It's so nice to meet you. I'm Eric, this is Leo.

Margaret Leo and I have already met. I thought we said eleven.

Eric We did, yes. I'm sorry we're / late.

Margaret It's half past noon.

Eric I know. I got distracted by the drive it's . . . I'm sorry for wasting your time.

Margaret No one wastes my time but me. I was telling Leo about this cherry tree.

Eric Yes, the teeth!

He goes to the tree, inspecting it.

Have you been taking care of the house for long?

Margaret I've been living in the area since 1989.

Eric So then you were you here when – ?

Margaret I was here when, yes.

Leo When what?

Margaret He doesn't know?

Eric I haven't told him yet.

Leo Told me what?

Margaret But he must know, he must understand.

Leo Understand what?

Margaret Leo, do you see that grove over there? In the distance, just beyond the meadow?

Leo Yes.

Margaret Once you're strong enough, we'll take a walk down there, the three of us. Through that grove, about fifty yards in, is a clearing where many men are buried.

Eric They're buried here?

Margaret Walter never told you that?

Leo What men? Who's buried there?

Margaret Years ago there was a plague. Do you know about it?

Leo Only a little.

Margaret And what little do you know about it?

Leo Many men died.

Margaret That could be said of any plague. What marked this as different?

Eric Many gay men died.

Margaret Thirty years ago, before you were born, we turned a blind eye to the deaths of tens of thousands of our fellow countrymen. In our disgust, we looked away, we made ourselves deaf to the cries of so many of our fellow citizens, of so many of our sons. Why were so many men allowed to die this way? I think it's because these men's illness required that Americans think about the means by which they contracted it. It required that we look at gay men and accept their nature, accept their affection and their desire for one another as equal to our own. Most Americans couldn't do that.

For years, men came to this house in need of care and Walter took them in. Men who were once so vital, wasted away to nothing. Men who were once so robust would have to be carried into the house. Walter could not heal their bodies but he tried to alleviate their suffering. He allowed them to leave this world with the kind of dignity they had long been denied while living in it.

I know this because one of the men who came here to die was my son.

Shall we go inside?

I wasn't given specific instructions. All Henry said was to take care of the things as I saw fit. It took nearly two weeks.

Eric Two weeks? Why so long?

Margaret You had a lot of things delivered.

Eric But the movers were told to leave them in the downstairs rooms.

Margaret Which they did. But then it was left to me to sort it all out.

Eric I don't understand. Sort what all out?

Margaret Your things.

Eric You unpacked my boxes?

Margaret Wasn't I supposed to?

Eric No. We were just storing my things here.

Margaret That was not made explicit.

Eric How much did you unpack?

Margaret All of it.

She unlocks the door, revealing once again the interior of the house. Only now the house is fully furnished.

Every book, every piece of furniture. Carpets, paintings,
photographs, knick-knacks. Sofas, end tables, lamps.
Bed and dressers. Dining table and chairs. Curtains
and drapes. Every room, upstairs and downstairs.

Eric And so, for the second time in his life, Eric entered
the house. He stood there dumbfounded as Margaret
began to open the shutters and then the windows, filling
the room with sunlight and air. There before him was his
life in possessions: his books . . . hundreds and hundreds
of them. The walls were covered with his artwork and
photographs. His old sofa and chairs and lamps and end
tables. He had not laid eyes on these things in almost two
years.

Margaret For a businessman, Henry can be maddeningly
imprecise. 'Make sure it all gets sorted out.' Those were
his words. 'Sorted out' does not mean 'stacked in a
corner gathering dust', 'Sorted out' means 'sorted out'.
Am I wrong?

Eric No. No, you're not.

Margaret And so . . . out it was sorted.

Margaret goes into the dining room, opening the
shutters and then the windows. The room fills with
sunlight.

Margaret There were some scratches in your dining
table. I did the best I could with it. It's a beautiful piece.

Eric It was my grandmother's.

Margaret Your grandmother had very good taste. I'm
envious of her china.

Eric Everything fits so perfectly.

Margaret This furniture belongs here. Like Walter did.
And you.

Eric Me?

Margaret You fit as perfectly here as the books on the shelf.

Leo You own a lot of books.

Margaret Yes, he does. I tried to instill some order. They'd been packed haphazardly. Fiction is alphabetized by author. Non-fiction by subject.

Eric I think I'm in love with you.

Margaret (*pointing up the stairs*) Shall we?

Eric nods. She heads up the stairs and he follows.
    Upstairs, Margaret opens the shutters in the bedrooms. Each of the rooms has a bed: a master bedroom with Eric's bedroom furniture and some smaller beds in the other rooms.

Eric Margaret, in all your time caring for this house, have you ever felt the presence of . . . I don't know how to say this without sounding completely insane . . .

Margaret You've seen them, haven't you?

A pause then . . .

Eric On my first visit. I thought maybe I was imagining things.

Margaret Walter told me about you, in the days before he passed. He said he had found someone he could leave this house to. You remind me of him in a way. I can't tell you how happy I am to know you'll be living here.

Eric Oh, no. I'm not going to be living here. I'm just here for a time. Just while Leo gets back to health.

Margaret You can think that if you want. But this is your home, Eric. You may not know it's yours, but it is. You're living here now and you have been since you stepped onto the land.

2. *Cemetery on Walter's Property*

Leo Eric and Leo had been at Walter's house for two weeks.

Eric Eric attended to Leo's physical, mental and spiritual health, starting him on the medications Eric's doctor prescribed. They made the first of several visits to a local, trusted dentist. One Sunday, Margaret took Leo and Eric to the graves of the men who had passed through the house long before them. Margaret showed them her son Michael's grave and told them stories about his childhood.

Margaret I was seventeen when I had him. Far too young to be given any responsibilities, let alone motherhood. News of my 'condition' was not met with joy. Had we been Catholics, we might have blamed it on immaculate conception. But we were Southern Baptists and so we blamed it on bourbon.

You've never seen a girl as frightened as I was the day Michael came into the world. I stared at him as he slept, I slipped my finger into his tiny hands, which he grabbed onto with such strength. That grip, that unwillingness to let go, astonished me. This helpless creature, encountering another human, gripping onto them and holding them tightly, as if fearing that to let go would risk never being held again. It was the first time in my life I understood that I was needed. It was the first time in my life I truly felt love.

Michael and I were both children when he was born. Only seventeen years apart in age. I don't think that I raised him so much as we raised each other. Michael saved me.

Michael was effeminate as a child. We called it 'sensitive'. Others had less compassionate words. I had less compassionate words. However, I cloaked them in faith. I would pray two things about Michael every night: God, please protect him. God, please don't let him be queer. I bought Michael a set of weights. He grew muscles. By the time Michael was eighteen and announced that he was moving to New York, he was six foot three and weighed two hundred and twenty pounds of pure, solid muscle. I sent him out into the world certain that, however effeminate he might be, at least his imposing physique would keep the queers away. What the hell did I know?

The night before he left, Michael and I stayed up late talking. I kept putting off sleep because I knew that the morning would bring with it his departure. I told him to find a church when he got there and to find himself a nice girl. Get in good with her family, I said. That way he'll be sure to get a decent meal every now and again. And then he told me – and I'll never forget the look of calm, knowing certainty in his eyes as he did – he told me there would be no girls for him, at least not in the way that I meant. 'Mama,' he said, 'I'm homosexual. I'm going to New York to fall in love.' This was more than I could bear to listen to. 'No,' I told him. 'You're confused. You're afraid. You're still so very young.'

In truth, I was the one who was afraid. Afraid of losing him. Afraid he'd be harmed. Afraid for his soul. I told him he could not be my son and be like that. I told him he would die of disease or violence. I told him he would spend eternity in hell. And do you know what he told me? That it was better than spending his life in South Carolina. I admire the moxy now but that night I wanted to hit him. My only consolation it is, that I didn't. But the damage had been done. I was no longer his mother, his protector, his one safe person in the world.

If I had known that night that he would only live another seven years, I would have held him in my arms and told him I loved him. I would have placed my hands inside his fist, just like I did when he was a baby. I would have comforted him, I would have recognized his desperate need for understanding and compassion. I would have shown him kindness.

But I didn't do that. I went to bed. I prayed and cried. By the time I woke the next morning, Michael was gone. I didn't see him again until the day he died.

We spoke intermittently over the years. Short, terse conversations over the phone. Christmas, Easter, my birthday. We never talked about his life. I never asked about his feelings or inquired about his heart. Several years went by when I did not speak to Michael at all.

Then one day, the telephone rang and a stranger's voice was on the line. He said his name was Walter Poole and that he was a friend of my son's. He was calling to tell me that Michael was sick and that Walter was taking care of him at his home in upstate New York. He didn't believe that Michael had long to live and said that if I wanted to visit I should come soon.

'Does he have it?' I asked.

'Yes,' Walter replied.

Walter opened the door for me and I walked inside. I climbed the stairs up to the bedroom where Michael lay. I did not know the man I saw there. I said as much to Walter and he assured me that this was Michael Timothy Avery, my son, aged twenty-five years. Asleep and breathing shallowly and hours away from death. My Michael.

His hair was short and brittle. His eyes were sunken. His face was covered in lesions. He looked older than I did. I stared at this pitiful creature before me, searching desperately for signs of my child.

I said to Walter: 'I haven't seen his face in seven years.'

And Walter asked me why I came.

'I came to tell him how angry I am at him.'

'Well,' Walter said, 'now's your chance.'

And I stared at my son, hours away from death, and I answered:

'I think he must know by now.'

I walked to his bed. I looked at his hands. The skin was dry. There was fungus growing under his nails. I slipped my hands into his, waiting for Michael to squeeze them as he once had.

I kept my vigil for seven hours. Walter brought me food but I didn't eat it. I couldn't move from Michael's side. The sun was starting to come up. Michael stirred. He opened his eyes. He smiled at me.

'Hi, Mom,' he said, his voice no more than a croak.

Michael closed his eyes. He squeezed my hand. I sat there for another hour as Michael faded, faded, faded away from me. His grip on my hands weakening until finally he stopped breathing and he slipped between my fingers and died.

Walter had befriended a man whose family owned a funeral home an hour from here. Gay, closeted. Terrified of being outed. And yet every time Walter called, this man would drive over, take each of the men and have them cremated. He'd return with the ashes and Walter would have a ceremony for them in this grove. We buried Michael's ashes alongside the others.

I went home the next day but I couldn't leave this place, not in my mind and not in my heart. I returned the next month and stayed with Walter.

More men came. Men like Michael, who had nowhere else to go. Over and over scenes like that played out in this house, as Walter and I did what we could to comfort these men. I held their hands as I held Michael's, as if they were my own child. I asked them about their pasts, their dreams that had been thwarted, their lives that had been interrupted and their futures that had been taken from me. Questions I should have spent seven years asking my son. Walter and I buried over two hundred men in this grove over the years.

Eric Two hundred?

Margaret There's a list of names somewhere upstairs. Walter knew all of them by heart. I regret I've started to forget them. But only their names. Never their faces. Those faces have stayed with me all these years, like ghosts. Michael's and so many others. A haunting, if you will. A necessary haunting.

Leo One evening, Margaret brought a photo album and showed them pictures of Michael as a child. Leo noticed how happy Michael seemed, always smiling brightly in every photo with Margaret. He could see in the boy's face a love he had never known as a child. When he told Margaret as much, she wept in his arms.

Eric Eric would wander the house and the property as Leo read beneath the cherry tree or baked pies with Margaret in the kitchen. He filled the house with wildflowers he had picked from the meadow. Leo grew stronger, the house once again exerting its healing presence and Eric waited for the moment Henry –

Margaret – or worse, his sons –

Leo Would arrive to throw them out.

Margaret But no one came except Margaret.

Leo And so, when Eric finally did hear a car pull up to the house one twilight, he understood that a reckoning had arrived. He simply had no idea which one.

End of Scene Two.

SCENE THREE

1. Walter's House

Toby enters, looking like utter hell. He holds a shopping bag in his hands. Eric steps out onto the porch. They stare at each other a few moments.

Toby I got lost along the way.

Your directions weren't very . . .

The house, it's . . . not easy to find.

I brought groceries. Also, a few bottles of '86 Margaux. And a hundred-year-old bottle of scotch. I can afford shit like that now.

Eric You look awful.

Toby Just . . . livin' the dream, baby.

He takes a step toward the house and loses his footing, collapsing to the ground. He decides to go with it and sits.

Eric I read your play. It's a complete mess.

Toby Who are you? Kenneth fuckin' Tynan all of a sudden?

Eric It's also the most courageous thing you've ever written. I know what it must've cost you.

Toby looks at Eric.

Toby I think my career is over.

Eric I think you've got more than just your career to worry about.

Toby I think you may be right.

Eric If it's any consolation, I think my marriage is over.

Toby has to think on that and then:

Toby I'm sorry.

Silence, then:
Eric goes into the house, leaving the door open. Toby stays on the ground, not sure what to do. Eric then comes back to the door.

Eric Come inside.

Toby gets to his feet and makes his way unsteadily inside the house.
Eric goes upstairs to Leo's room, knocks and enters. Eric sits on Leo's bed, pulls Leo close to him and whispers into Leo's ear. Leo reacts in fear and anguish.
As this is happening, Toby enters the house, starts looking around.

Toby Holy shit, it's all our things. Your things. I didn't realize you were living here.
All your books.
That's a great view. That meadow is beautiful.

Eric returns. Leo is with him.

Eric Toby . . .

Toby turns in shocked silence, to see Leo standing there. But then –

Toby Adam? What the fuck are you doing here?

It is as if Leo has been punched in the stomach. He runs off. Toby looks at Eric.

Eric That isn't Adam, Toby.

Toby, realizing his terrible mistake, begins to implode.
Leo re-enters, a glass of water in his hand. He charges at Toby, throws the water in Toby's face and smashes the glass over Toby's head. Both Toby's head and Leo's hands are cut and bleeding.
Toby falls to the ground. Leo advances on him to continue the attack – when Eric grabs Leo and stops him. Leo cries as Eric holds him tightly in his arms, whispering calming, loving words insistently into his ear. Words only Leo can hear. Eric allows Leo to sob as he holds him tightly.

2. *Walter's House*

Later that night. Toby on the porch, drunk. Eric steps outside.

Toby I should go.

Eric You're in no condition to drive.

Toby I don't know what to do, Eric. Please tell me what to do.

Eric You looked at the wrong part of yourself when you wrote that play. You looked at the part of you that's damaged. But what about the part of you that's good?

Toby I don't think that part exists anymore. I don't know if it ever did.

Eric The day I met you, I remember thinking, 'This guy is a lot, but this guy is alive.' You shone with life, with promise. And all I wanted was to be next to you for as long as I could.

Toby I hurt you very badly, didn't I?

Eric More than anyone ever has.

Toby But you kept loving me anyway.

Eric Go talk to him.

Toby I wouldn't know what to say.

Eric Start with the truth.

Toby I don't . . . I can't . . . I don't know what the truth is anymore.

Then:

Eric There is a box in the attic filled with your parents' things. Maybe it's time you opened it.

3. Walter's House

Eric Late that night, after both Eric and Leo had fallen asleep, Toby opened his hundred-year-old bottle of scotch and took it with him to the attic and opened the box Eric had been storing for him for almost two years.

Toby Envelopes stuffed with family photos, his early writing, movie tickets. Trinkets. (*He picks up a photo.*) His mother, once so young and beautiful. (*Then another photo.*) His father, forever young, robust and handsome. (*Then another photo.*) Toby then finds a photo of himself at seven years old, two months before his father died. He is standing in his pajamas, his eyes staring directly at the camera. So sweet, so unformed and so trusting. This young boy's only request of the world is that he be loved. He has no idea that life as he knows it will end in two months' time. Toby stares at the photo, searching for himself in his seven-year-old face. He cannot find it. It is as if Toby were looking at a stranger. The loved boy in the photo bears no resemblance to the lost man who is holding it. This beautiful boy could never have done all the damage that Toby has done. This innocent child could never have hurt all the people that Toby has. And in that moment, Toby knows that he can never heal, that he was only built to destroy. The poison is too deep inside him for the antidote to work. Toby grabs a pencil and a piece of paper and quickly scrawls across it. He grabs his keys and flees the house. Toby careens down the empty thruway. Eighty, then ninety, then one hundred miles an hour. And in that last second as his car hurtles toward the concrete wall, Toby wishes he had told Leo how much he –

Leo In the morning, Eric goes to the attic and finds Toby's note. Its message encapsulated in two words:

Eric 'I can't.'

Leo Later that morning, a phone call. Eric and Leo are told of an accident on the southbound side of the thruway. A single car, upside down in flames. And inside of it, Toby Darling, who could not heal. Burned alive by the fire that consumed him long before help was called, a lifetime before help arrived.

End of Scene Three.

SCENE FOUR

1. *Cemetery on Walter's Property*

Young Man 1 They buried Toby's ashes in the small cemetery on Walter's property.

Young Man 8 It was not the funeral Toby had imagined in his darker fantasies.

Young Man 5 There were no celebrities in attendance, no great speeches were given.

Young Man 2 The Jasons drove up from the city.

Young Man 7 Jasper did as well.

Young Man 3 Henry returned from Riyadh.

Young Man 6 Tristan flew in from Toronto.

Young Man 1 Adam sent flowers.

Eric Eric read from Toby's early writing and then, one by one, they bid their friend farewell.

Young Man 6 Eric, as was his nature, made lunch for everyone.

Young Man 1 It was a fine spring day. The house was once again full of people.

2. *Walter's House*

Eric and Henry.

Henry I have to go back to Saudi tomorrow. It can't be helped.

Eric I understand. Thank you for coming. I know how hard it is for you to be here.

Henry I assume you and . . . I assume you and Leo plan to stay here a little longer.

Eric We do.

Henry I shouldn't be gone more than two weeks.

Eric I'm not coming back to you, Henry.

Henry Eric.

Eric Because I know you'd do everything in your power to make this pain go away.

Henry Yes, of course I would. And why shouldn't I?

Eric Because I don't want it to go away. I have to put it to some use or else all of this will have been pointless.

Henry But there is no point to suffering.

Eric There is if you can learn from it. And I do want to learn from it.

Henry No, you want to torture yourself.

Eric I want to feel things! I want to stop running from the things that frighten me.

Henry Don't you see that this is running away? This is where I came to be lost to the world.

Eric And don't you see that this is where I've come to live in the world?

Henry Eric, please.

After a hesitation:

I know that I haven't always . . . I haven't said the things I know you've needed to hear. I've spent the last year trying to find a way to tell you. Maybe I just needed to say the words. I need you, Eric.

I love you.

Eric I love you too, Henry. I do. I was with you because I wanted to be. But I married you because I was afraid not to.

Henry Please don't leave me.

Eric I'm sorry, Henry. But if I don't do this, I'm afraid I'll never do anything again.

Silence.

I have one thing to ask of you. I know I have no right to, but . . . I wondered if you would be willing to give me this house.

A chill crawls up Henry's spine.

Young Man 3 And here we are again –

Henry – back where we started.

Eric What do you mean?
Henry?

Eventually . . .

Henry When Walter was ill, after you had been so kind to him, he wrote your name down on a piece of paper indicating that he wanted you to have his house. I decided at the time . . . I decided it wasn't . . . that it couldn't have been Walter's true desires. So I set it aside. I ignored his wishes, never knowing what you'd come to mean to me in time. And not knowing that Walter had known all along what was best for this house, and what was best for you.

Silence. Eric seems to be shaken in his innermost recesses.

Eric Why did you tell me that?

Henry Because no man should ever have to ask for that which is rightfully his.

3. Obituaries

Margaret And for the second time in as many years, Eric Glass said goodbye to a partner and began his life anew.

Young Man 5 Unbeknownst to Eric, Toby had named him the executor of his literary estate.

Young Man 8 He never once saw Toby's play in the two years it ran on Broadway, nor when it was revived off-Broadway thirty years later.

Young Man 7 Three years after Toby's death, Eric authorized the publication of his last play. Finally, the world understood who Toby Darling really was.

Young Man 6 Five years after Toby's death and his divorce from Henry, Eric met the man who would become the love of his life.

Young Man 3 They were married at Eric's house upstate, Leo serving as Eric's best man.

Young Man 2 Eric found his path in life by illuminating it for others.

Young Man 4 Without ever planning to, Eric became a teacher, a mentor, and eventually a wise old man to so many who encountered him.

Eric Eric's life was filled with love, with friendship, with family.

Margaret Eric Glass died at the age of ninety-seven at his beloved house in upstate New York. He fell asleep one night while reading in front of the fire and never woke up.

Young Man 6 He was buried next to his husband in the cemetery on his property, and among the countless men who had died there nearly a century before during the time of the plague.

Young Man 8 Eric's three children, seven grandchildren and fourteen great-grandchildren inherited the house, which they maintain to this day as a cherished family home.

Young Man 4 And what of the young man Leo?

Young Man 1 Leo stayed at Walter's house – now Eric's – for six months after Toby's death.

Young Man 7 He was healthy and strong. And while his body was quick to heal, his spirit moved slowly toward recovery.

Young Man 3 He received his GED and enrolled in college.

Young Man 1 Eric paid his tuition from the income he received from Toby's royalties.

Young Man 5 There wasn't a Christmas or a Thanksgiving the two did not spend together for many years.

Young Man 2 When he was forty, Leo met the man who would become his partner for the next twenty-seven years.

Eric Leo rarely felt alone, for he seldom was.

Young Man 1 And, in his later years, when sickness returned or when sadness visited, Leo would think of his life and conjure immense feelings of gratitude for all those he had loved and been loved by.

Margaret Leo died in Eric's house, in the room where he always stayed, the room where Walter's friend Peter and Margaret's son Michael had died decades earlier. He was sixty-seven, an age too young by most standards but far older than he ever imagined he'd see. Leo died holding Eric's hand, listening to the sound of the breeze rustling through the curtains. The house stood then as it had for centuries and would for centuries more: as a shelter, a refuge, a place of healing; a reminder of the pain, the fragility, and the promise of life.

End of Act Three.

Epilogue

1. *Eric's House*

It is late afternoon on a brilliant autumn day. The cherry tree is aflame in brilliant red and orange leaves. The sun filters through them, casting a golden glow on the house and property.

The yard is festooned with lights and balloons. Off in the distance, the sound of a wonderful party: people talking, laughing, music playing. There's a magical quality in the air.

Leo enters. He approaches the house, having just arrived. He holds a gift bag in his hands. He stares at the house lovingly. Eric enters from inside the house. He sees Leo and rushes to him, pulling him tightly into an embrace.

Eric You made it!

Leo Sorry I'm late. I got a late start and then traffic / was –

Eric You're here now, that's all that matters.

Leo Happy birthday!

Eric Thank you.

Leo You're forty!

Eric Shhh . . . maybe no one will notice.

Leo I have something for you.

Eric Is it what I think it is?

Leo It is. Although I feel it's a little self-serving as a gift.

Eric No. It's the greatest gift you could ever give me.

Leo hands over the gift bag and Eric pulls out a bound manuscript.

Your first novel. I'm so proud of you.

He looks at the cover.

'The Inheritance'.

Leo Read the dedication.

Eric flips to it and reads:

Eric 'For Eric, who saved me.'
Thank you, Leo.

Eric then flips to the first page.

Leo Don't read it now!

Eric Just the first page. (*Reading.*) 'One may as well begin with Toby's voicemails to his boyfriend.'

Leo I didn't change his name. I just . . . it didn't feel right to.

Eric I think that's okay. It's the truth.

Eric closes the manuscript, looking at it.

Oh Toby . . .

Leo wraps an arm around Eric.

I promised myself I wouldn't cry today and I meant it. I've shed many tears for the dead and I will shed many more before I'm through. But not today.

Henry enters.

Henry Am I interrupting?

Eric Leo was just showing me his book.

Henry Have you finished?

Leo I sent it to my publisher on Friday.

Eric hands Henry the manuscript.

Henry My goodness. Congratulations. Am I in it?

Leo Yes, but I changed your name.

Henry Good idea.

Leo I called you 'Henry Wilcox', like in *Howards End*.

Henry I think Walter would have approved.
Mr Glass?

Eric Yes, Mr Wilcox?

Henry Everyone is waiting for you. We can't have a
birthday dinner without the guest of honor.

Eric Right.

Eric takes Leo's hand.

Come on, I can't wait to hear what you've been up to.
We have so many stories to tell each other.

*Eric and Leo start to go off together. Eric turns to face
Henry.*

Eric Aren't you coming, Henry?

Henry I'm actually a little chilly. Do you mind if I borrow
a sweater?

Eric Not at all. You should find something in the top
drawer of my dresser.

Leo Did you finish the dining pavilion?

Eric Yes! It's going to be breathtaking at Thanksgiving.

*Eric and Leo run off toward the party. Henry stands in
place, watching them go.*

He then opens the manuscript and begins flipping through until he finds a passage with his name in it. He reads:

Henry 'Henry was caught by the sight of the house. To see it alive once again, the lights inside glowing warmly through the windows. The sound of the voices and music filling the air. The late afternoon light diffused in the brilliant autumn leaves of the grand old cherry tree. How could Walter have known, how could he have seen how things would inevitably be? Henry looked all around him. For the first time he truly saw the beauty of it. Not the property itself, although the property was beautiful. No, what Henry saw was the beauty of his life. A life blessed by this house and Walter and Eric and all his friends both living and long dead. Finally . . .'

As he reads, Leo has quietly re-entered with a sweater. He stands back, listening. Then gently makes his presence known. Henry looks over at him.

Leo 'Finally in that moment, Henry saw it all. The past, the present and the future all at once, all in concert, all around him.'
Eric asked me to bring you this.

Henry hands Leo the book and takes the sweater.

Henry Thank you.

Henry looks around at the property, puts on the sweater. As he does:
    Walter appears.

Walter Maybe we should plant some bluebells around the perimeter of the house. Or peonies.

Henry is struck by the sight of him. Then:

Henry How about both?

Walter I can't believe we own this. I can't believe all this is ours.

Henry We will be so happy here, I promise.

Walter I believe you, Henry. How could we not be? I should probably get dinner started.

Henry No, stay with me. Dinner can wait.

Walter You say that now.

He starts to leave.

Henry Walter.
Forgive me. Please forgive me, Walter. I'm so, I'm so sorry. I wasted so much time.

Walter You have so much left.

Henry What do I do now, Walter? Tell me what to do.

Walter You do what they could not.

He lovingly takes Henry's face in his hands and kisses him deeply.

You live.

The stage floods with golden light. The house glows intensely.
  Then black.

End of Play.